ecpr PRESS

I0091228

Split-Ticket Voting in Mixed-Member Electoral Systems

A Theoretical and Methodological Investigation

Carolina Plescia

ecprPRESS

First published by the ECPR Press in 2016

The ECPR Press is the publishing imprint of the European Consortium for Political Research (ECPR), a scholarly association, which supports and encourages the training, research and cross-national co-operation of political scientists in institutions throughout Europe and beyond.

ECPR Press
Harbour House
Hythe Quay
Colchester
CO2 8JF
United Kingdom

Typeset by Lapiz Digital Services

Printed and bound by Lightning Source

British Library Cataloguing in Publication Data

A catalogue record for this book is available from the British Library

HARDBACK ISBN: 978-1-785521-80-5
PAPERBACK ISBN: 978-1-785522-59-8
PDF ISBN: 978-1-785521-81-2
EPUB ISBN: 978-1-785521-82-9
KINDLE ISBN: 978-1-785521-83-6

www.ecpr.eu/ecprpress

More in the ECPR Press Monographs series

Between Nationalism and Europeanisation
(ISBN 9781785521430) Nevena Nancheva

Visions of Judicial Review
(ISBN: 9781785521478) Benjamin Bricker

Europeanised or European?
(ISBN: 9781785522321) Sandra Kröger

Situating Governance
(ISBN: 9781907301681) Antonino Palumbo

A Responsive Technocracy?
(ISBN: 9781785521270) Christian Rauh

Please visit http://www.ecpr.eu/ecprpress for information about new publications.

Contents

Contents

List of Figures and Tables

Figures

Tables

List of Abbreviations

2x2 tables	Contingency tables with two rows and two columns
EI-MD	Ecological Inference- Multinomial Dirichlet method
EI-ML	Ecological Inference- Multinomial Logistic method
PR	Proportional tier of the ballot paper
PR-STV	Proportional Single Transferable Vote system
Root-MSE	Root-Mean Squared Error
RxC tables	Contingency tables with more than two rows and two columns
SMD	Single Member District tier of the ballot paper
SNTV	Single Non-Transferable Vote system

Acknowledgements

This study builds on my dissertation work. It was only possible because of the help and support of many people, who I have now the pleasure to thank.

First and foremost my PhD supervisors, Prof. Kenneth Benoit and Prof. Michael Marsh, who gave me the opportunity of pursuing my research under their guidance and then supported me throughout the years with enduring patience and precious advice. I thank Ken who guided this project from its beginning providing useful comments and suggestions. I am grateful to Michael Marsh who took over the supervision of my PhD thesis in 2011. Through his guidance my PhD thesis has changed and improved and his insight and support over these years have been invaluable.

I also owe a debt of gratitude to the faculty of Trinity College's Department of Political Science for their input, to my friends and colleagues in the PhD program for their help and support during my time at Trinity, and to the Institute for International Integration Studies (IIIS) for the hospitality. The department of Political Science in Trinity College, Dublin provides an excellent and stimulating research environment. I wish to thank in particular my friends and colleagues Silvia Caló, Ed Coughlan, Michael Courtney, Koji Kagotani, Caroline McEvoy, Natalie Novick, Alan Power, Kristin Semancik and Magdalena Staniek. Thanks are due to Prof. Daniela Giannetti, my teacher and my mentor, who prompted the start of this project and provided support every time I needed it. Her encouragement set me on track. I would also like to thank the Methodology Institute and the Department of Government at the London School of Economics for the hospitality during my stay as a visiting student in 2012.

This project received generous financial support by the Irish Research Council for the Humanities and Social Sciences (IRCHSS) and the PhD scholarship provided by Trinity College Dublin. The simulations presented in Chapters Three, Five and Six of this book were performed on the Lonsdale cluster maintained by the Trinity Centre for High Performance Computing. This cluster was funded through grants from Science Foundation Ireland. In addition, for replication material in Chapter Three of this book I gratefully acknowledge the assistance of Profs. Martin Elff, Roy Johnston and Kevin Quinn. For support with collection of data for New Zealand I thank Prof. Jack Vowel, for Scotland I thank Prof. John Curtice and for Japan I thank in particular Dr. Yuki Yanai.

I also received helpful feedback from audiences in various venues, including conferences participants at the Graduate Conference of the European Consortium of Political Research (ECPR) 2009; at the Annual Conference of the Italian Political Science Association 2011; at the Annual Conference of the European Political Science Association 2012 and 2013; at the General Conference of the True European Voter (TEV) 2013 and at the Internal Seminar series at the

Department of Methods in the Social Sciences, Vienna University. Of course, all remaining errors are mine.

A big thanks goes to those who have been close, even from a distance: all my friends and, of course, my parents and my brother who made it all possible. They taught me how rewarding hard work can be and their love and support have made me believe I can accomplish anything. Lastly, and most importantly, I would like to thank Paolo the constant source of technical advice and firm encouragement who gave me strength when I needed it the most. I am sure that I wouldn't be where I am had it not been for him. This book is dedicated to him.

PART I

SPLIT-TICKET VOTING: DEFINITION AND MEASUREMENT

Chapter One

Introduction: What is it and Why Study Split-Ticket Voting?

This book contributes to the literature on electoral behaviour by analysing vote choice in mixed-member electoral systems (hereafter referred to as mixed systems). Mixed systems give individuals the opportunity to vote for the same representative body by casting two votes: one for a national party and one for a local candidate. The two votes are subject to two electoral formulas: proportional for the party vote (hereafter referred to as PR vote) and majoritarian for the candidate vote (hereafter referred to as SMD vote) (Gallagher and Mitchell 2005: 591). Under some mixed systems, voters receive two separate ballot papers, one with a list of candidates and one with a list of parties (e.g., Hungary, Russia, and Scotland). In some other cases, voters find the parties and candidates listed on the same ballot paper (e.g., Germany, New Zealand, Venezuela). In rare cases, such as in Mexico, voters cast only one vote. This, however, is subject to double counting, for the party and for the party's candidate. In mixed-member electoral systems, voters are said to cast a 'straight ticket' if the local candidate they vote for belongs to the same party for which they cast their proportional vote; otherwise, they are said to cast a 'split-ticket vote'.[1]

At the heart of this study is a narrow question: why, in mixed-member electoral systems, do citizens split their vote by choosing a party and then a candidate affiliated with a different party? This book shows that the answer to this question is more nuanced than one might expect. Indeed, the manner in which voters split their ticket offers observable implications on a wide range of theoretical explanations of voting behaviour including personalisation of politics, voters' ability to strategically work within the institutions of representative democracy, as well as the effect of institutions and political structures on how people vote. Mixed systems offer a natural laboratory to investigate these research questions due to the presence of two votes (the party and the candidate vote) cast under two distinct electoral rules (proportional and majoritarian) to elect the same legislative body. Using Moser and Scheiner (2004: 576) words: 'mixed electoral systems represent a social laboratory in which effects of different types of electoral systems can be studied in isolation from influences of the social context such as social cleavages, socioeconomic development, or culture'.

---

1. Voting for different parties in simultaneous elections has been defined using other labels such as 'vote switching', 'ticket-splitting', 'divided voting', 'vote shifts' and 'floating voter' amongst others.

Furthermore, the measurement of split-ticket voting posits a methodological challenge: the secret ballot hinders the possibility of measuring split-ticket voting directly and researchers must infer its occurrence using individual-level surveys or aggregate-level data. Each approach is limited and the use of either type of data usually relies on voting behaviour assumptions that are seldom testable. Leveraging on a wealth of data, this book relaxes these common assumptions and tests current empirical measurements. As the measurement issues plaguing the study of split-ticket voting are quite common in studies of vote choice, a methodological analysis of split-ticket voting has the potential to provide insights for the study of electoral behaviour more generally. The book proposes new approaches with which to investigate split-ticket voting as well as a new answer to the 'why' of vote-splitting.

This study employs a number of innovations to answer the 'why' question. First, it takes a nuanced approach that does not rely on the existing literature's intuitive assumptions, but on real behaviour where it can be measured and evaluated. The book undermines assumptions such as party-centred voting and challenges the current understanding of strategic split-ticket voting to develop an original understanding of vote choice under mixed rules. Second, the book uses both individual and aggregate-level data and proves that a composite approach provides a more accurate understanding of split-ticket voting. Third, the book uses a comparative rather than a more common case study approach to study split-ticket voting. Cross-national comparison is essential since the generalisations based on one specific country experience may be inapplicable to other cases. This may be due to specific country-level factors such as prior experience with the electoral rules; levels of party institutionalisation may alter voters' propensity and capacity to act on certain incentives provided by the electoral rules. In addition, specifics of the electoral rules may alter the incentives to engage in specific behaviours. The two additional case studies of Japan and Italy focus on distinct settings which allow me to confirm and expand some of the findings derived from the comparative analysis.

The puzzle

Where parties dominate government and the nominations of candidates for legislative office, the fact that so many voters do not appear to structure their electoral choice by one party, presents something of a puzzle. The elections in the United States of America (US) are normally arranged in such a way that many offices are filled at the same time, with electors choosing occupants for a wide range of offices on one day. Most voters pick a president, a congressman and more, all from the same party, choosing to vote a straight ticket. However, some do not, opting instead for a split ticket with, perhaps, a Republican for President and a Democrat for the Senate (e.g., Roscoe 2003; Burden and Kimball 2004). Similarly, in mixed systems, and where scholarly investigations exist, findings illustrate that many voters actually cross party lines when choosing their representatives (e.g., Karp *et al.* 2002; Johnston and Pattie 2003; Gschwend *et al.* 2003). As well as being theoretically intriguing, such behaviour may be substantively important as it has consequences for election outcomes (e.g., Benoit *et al.* 2006; Burden and Helmke 2009).

In the US, two broad theoretical viewpoints have been offered to explain patterns of split-ticket voting. The distinguishing feature between these two approaches is whether voters are seen as acting strategically or sincerely. Several scholars posit that US voters split intentionally to achieve a divided party government, a situation in which one party controls the executive branch and another party controls one or both houses of the Congress, the legislative branch (Alesina and Rosenthal 1995; Fiorina 1992). The opposing camp finds no support for these strategic motivations and proposes alternative explanations (e.g., Alvarez and Schousen 1993; Beck *et al.* 1992; Mattei and Howes 2000). In a nutshell, this second line of research argues that split-ticket voting in the US can be accounted for largely by forces specific to a particular context, such as the polarisation of the district races and specific traits of competing candidates (Roscoe 2003, Burden and Kimball 2004). After more than 70 years of research what causes Americans to split their tickets is still unsettled.

The arguments are a little different in the study of mixed-member electoral systems where split-ticket voting tends to be seen as strategic, as opposed to straight ticket that is often regarded as sincere voting. The majority of the existing studies argue that voters have strong incentives to deviate from voting for a candidate in the majoritarian tier of the ballot paper when that party's candidate has no chance of winning the election (Bawn 1999; Karp *et al.* 2002) but may nonetheless support that candidate's party with their proportional vote. Furthermore, in line with an emerging literature emphasising the possibility of strategic voting under proportional rules (Bargsted and Kedar 2009; Hobolt and Karp 2010; Abramson *et al.* 2010), scholars have recognised the possibility that supporters of strong parties may split strategically in favour of a junior coalition partner on the proportional ballot to help the smaller party cross the electoral threshold (Gschwend 2007).

Yet, there are many conceivable reasons as to why voters may deviate from their most preferred party, and thus cast a split vote, for reasons other than strategic ones. Some of these alternatives, such as personal voting and the structure of opportunities faced by voters, have attracted less attention in studies of vote choice under mixed systems and continue to be debated. These alternatives are consistent with split-ticket voting but derive from micro-level, non-strategic reasons. The literature acknowledges the existence of alternative explanations for a type of voting behaviour that is observationally equivalent to a strategically motivated split-ticket (Schoen 1999; Pappi and Thurner 2002: 212). However, with very few exceptions, discussed below, existing studies provide no more than anecdotal evidence on the adequacy of these explanations of split-ticket voting. I argue here that these alternatives deserve closer examination, especially because of their potential to shed light on the increasingly weak bond between voters and parties in many mature democracies. Similarly, straight-ticket voting, which is often considered a sign of sincere voting, may be strategic. For instance, an adherent of a very small party that has no chance of entering the parliament may decide to cast a strategic straight ticket for a larger party instead. It is clear that drawing conclusions about strategic and sincere voting from observed behaviour is highly problematic.

These unsettled issues concerning a widespread citizens' practice of crossing party lines when casting a vote bring up numerous questions pertaining to principles of voting behaviour as well as to parties' electoral strategies. The general underlying question is: what is the logic of vote choice under mixed rules? To answer this question, I test several proposed explanations as well as review the methods used to analyse these explanations. The focus is on voters' preferences and motivations, as well as on the way different institutional environments may lead voters to employ different decision rules.

What is new

The literature on electoral politics in general, and on voter choice in particular, is vast. This book builds on insights from previous studies to yield new ones. First, I focus on what voters are concerned with when casting a vote and the tension between preferences and outcomes. The study of strategic voting is based on the broad idea that voters are concerned with the impact of their vote on the electoral outcome. It focuses on party preferences and defines a vote that contradicts pure party-centred reasoning as strategic. The assumption of party-centred reasoning, however, is particularly problematic in mixed-member electoral systems given that voters vote simultaneously for parties and candidates and one should recognise that some voters may start by choosing a majoritarian candidate and follow the candidate to a party with the party vote. In extremely party-oriented election systems, like Italy's or Germany's, it may be fair to assume that most voters start with at least a loose attachment to a party, but in countries with a highly personalistic nature of the political system, such as Japan (Reed 2003), or in countries where new parties form and disappear frequently, and where many voters are non-aligned, such voters may be in a minority.

Following this reasoning, this project does not negate voters' ability to act strategically. Rather, it relaxes the party-centred vote assumption by adding to the usual picture of voters voting for parties other considerations; in particular I focus on the effect on vote choice of candidates' preferences and candidates' availability on the electoral ballot. The project clearly shows that an explanation of strategic voting has to go beyond the consideration of party preferences and incorporate the separate preferences that voters may have for parties and candidates. At the same time, the actual presence of voters' preferred option on the ballot paper must be accounted for. The common assumption that voters vote primarily for parties is not only unrealistic but also theoretically problematic. I will show that the reliance on these assumptions can potentially overestimate the importance of strategic voting and underestimate the influence of voters' *true* preferences on vote choice. The logic put forth in this study reinterprets the debate between the standard account of strategic and personal vote as well as identifying conditions under which they are likely to emerge.

Second, unlike many studies of voting behaviour, this study, while focusing on individuals, examines the logic voters employ as one that is embedded in, affected by, and reflective of particular political contexts. Most mixed systems are quite unique and cover a heterogeneous array of electoral systems. Given their focus on single-case study, existing studies failed to embed micro-level reasoning into the particular institutional conditions. Yet we know that different electoral rules have an impact on vote choice in different ways, starting from the very availability of candidates on the ballot paper. In particular, this book provides the first cross-country analysis of vote choice under mixed systems using both individual and aggregate-level data. In doing so, it integrates institutional contexts into the analysis of voter choice.

Lastly, this project speaks to the literature on vote choice from a methodological point of view, revisiting issues of measurement and the debate between the use of individual and aggregate-level data to study vote choice. There are various ways to measure split-ticket voting – each with its own shortcomings. Measuring why people split their vote using surveys has usually relied on untested assumptions about the centrality of party preferences on vote choice. An alternative measure involves the use of aggregate electoral results. When relying on aggregate data, the existing literature uses the net measure of split-ticket voting, calculating the difference between the votes gained by the party and the affiliated candidate in a certain district. This measure of the dependent variable is, however, flawed by significant problems as it only provides the minimum level of split-ticket voting that actually takes place and it is not able to account for all the cross-voting among parties and candidates (Cowart 1974; King 1997). I review these methodological limitations in Chapter Three and point to improvements on the use of both types of data. Beyond that, the project shows that it is ultimately the combination of individual and aggregate-level data, i.e. surveys and electoral results, which enable a comprehensive study of vote choice. In general, while I answer the research question of why voters split their vote focusing on mixed-member electoral systems, the book has the final aim of explaining the choice people make on the Election Day and contributes to its measurement and understanding.

Data and methods

The book leverages individual and aggregate level data in an attempt to develop a unified account that features specific cross-polity flavours. Given that I am primarily interested in the micro-logic of why people split their vote, I predominantly use survey data and the focus in every chapter lies on a particular country and often on a particular election. Notwithstanding, the conclusions drawn at the end of each chapter have a bird's eye view on the analysis, at both the individual and aggregate level. The aggregate level data decomposed at the constituency level enables a discussion of the variation of split-ticket voting across sub-national geographical units in each country. The individual level focuses on the behaviour and attitudes of voters. The two complement each other and it is their interplay that enables the bird's eye conclusions. This is done to take into account the impact of voters' preferences and motivations, as well as the effects of district factors on the way people vote.

The comparative analysis instead focuses explicitly on institutional-level variation to draw conclusions on how, and if, types of mixed systems affect individual-level vote choice. There are two main types of mixed systems: mixed-proportional and mixed-majoritarian. The former are almost pure systems of proportional representation. By contrast, in mixed-majoritarian systems, the two tiers of the electoral system are completely separate as regards to the allocation of seats. This provision strongly limits the proportionality of the system (Gallagher and Mitchell 2005: 592). The types of mixed rules have the potential of influencing vote choice by altering the incentives that citizens face when casting their vote (e.g., Moser and Scheiner 2005; Gschwend 2007), as more extensively explained below.

Split-ticket voting can be studied at the individual as well as at the aggregate level. At the individual level, the classical dependent variable in studies of vote choice under mixed-member systems is a dummy variable which takes a value of 0 when the voters cast a vote for the local candidate belonging to the same party for which they cast their proportional vote and 0 otherwise. This book departs from the existing literature by altering the measurement of both the dependent variable and the independent variables. On the former, the dependent variable is not split-ticket voting as such but vote choice examined separately in the two parts of the ballot paper. This is done while providing a comparative investigation drawing upon nine country-studies including national elections in Albania, Germany, Hungary, Italy, Japan, New Zealand, Thailand, South Korea, and the sub-state elections in Scotland. These countries enable us to cover all possible instances of mixed rules, mixed-proportional and mixed-majoritarian systems. These countries also allow variation on several additional dimensions, such as familiarity with the electoral rules and experience with the representative democracy.

Another departure from the existing literature is to analyse split-ticket voting using the classical dummy variable straight/split vote but this time by changing the operationalisation of the independent variables. Instead of building the independent variables, as is usually done in the existing literature, by considering the vote as being party-centred; all variables are measured *also* starting from the candidate. For instance, the standard practice of identifying the most preferred party uses a feeling thermometer question to build a variable, taking a value of 1 if the respondent ranks highest the party voted for on the proportional tier and 0 otherwise. In this book this classical measure is compared to a candidate-centred measure whereby the most preferred party variable takes a value of 1 if the respondent ranks highest the party of the candidate supported on the majoritarian tier and 0 otherwise. The central aim is to check whether or not voters consider the two votes similarly and to examine the extent of which the commonly used variables specification provides different substantial results to an alternative candidate-centred specification. This is done focusing on two case studies, the Japanese lower house elections and the Italian regional elections, spanning all elections since the introduction of the mixed rules. These two cases enable us to answer additional questions left unanswered from the comparative analysis.

At the aggregate level, the current literature uses official electoral results to measure split-ticket voting as the 'candidate vote gap'. The vote gap is obtained by measuring the difference between the votes for the party and those for the linked candidate in a certain district. A negative vote gap has always been understood as meaning that the candidate did worse than his party and a positive gap that the candidate did better. This net measure of split-ticket voting is, however, severely limited by the ecological inference problem. Indeed, the candidate vote gap can only report the minimum level of split-ticket voting that actually takes place because all the cross-votes among parties and candidates cancel each other out (Gschwend *et al.* 2003). Specifically, although a substantial amount of net split-ticket voting at the party level must reflect at least an equally large switching at the individual level, the reverse does not hold: small, even zero, net split-ticket voting can be the product of considerable, but self-cancelling vote-switching at the individual level. Because of the methodological limitations of the candidate vote gap, existing analyses based on aggregate data provide, for the most part, potentially biased results. One available solution to this puzzle lies in using indirect methods to obtain estimates of split-ticket voting.

The book first tests and then uses more advanced methods for the measurement of the split-ticket voting at the aggregate level. To run these tests I employed data from the national elections in New Zealand and the sub-state elections in Scotland. I chose these two countries as testing settings because for them, exceptionally, data on *true* party-level split-ticket voting are ready available. The true amount of split-ticket voting by party at the district level is generally unknown. Because in these two contexts the true level of vote switching is known, it is possible to empirically evaluate the performance and accuracy of indirect methods of estimation before employing them to study substantively the variation of split-ticket voting in other countries. Disaggregated quantities of district-level split-ticket voting by party can then be used as a dependent variable in regression models to investigate variation of split-ticket voting across parties, as well as across districts.

To sum up, individual and aggregate-level data provide insights on different phenomena and they complement each other. Surveys provide unique access to voters' preferences and motivations and their use provides insights in to why people split their vote; I focus on voters' preferences and motivations as well as on cross-country variation. The study is however expanded by an analysis of split-ticket voting at the aggregate level focused on party and district-level variation. For this last investigation one needs aggregate data since surveys do not usually provide information that is representative of all the districts inside a country (Gschwend *et al.* 2003; Johnston and Pattie 2003).

The road ahead: structure of the book

To the best of my knowledge this book represents the first systematic study of split-ticket voting at both the aggregate and individual level by using a comparative approach. In my journey, I move back and forth between the micro- and the macro-level and spend time understanding micro-fundamental principles that guide voters, as well as the effect that the types of mixed rules have on vote choice. To this aim, the book combines a purely methodological analysis based on the New Zealand and Scottish elections, with substantial investigations comprising a comparative study, and two in-depth case studies of Japan and Italy. The purpose of this book is thus twofold. First, the book aims to provide a substantial advancement of the current literature on split-ticket voting, testing its assumptions and findings. In addition, the book has the methodological purpose of testing the use of surveys and aggregate-level data for the study of split-ticket voting. The final aim of this investigation is to provide new insights on the causes and instances of vote choice under mixed rules and to contribute to the broader literature on voting behaviour.

This book consists of three parts. The first part includes three chapters. Chapter One explains the motivations for research and discusses how the study of split-ticket voting relates to our knowledge of voting behaviour more generally. Chapter Two reviews the literature presenting the theoretical foundations of this project and how it contributes to it. Chapter Three is devoted to the measurement of the dependent variable: split-ticket voting. Part II of the book presents the empirical results based on a cross-country analysis (Chapter Four), a case study of candidates and split-ticket voting in Japan (Chapter Five), and a study of pre-electoral coalitions and split-ticket voting in Italy (Chapter Six). Part III of the book includes a conclusion chapter, appendices and the bibliography. The study ends with the theoretical questions about citizens' preferences and motivations as well as the extent to which parties and candidates shape voting behaviour and influence the working of electoral democracy.

Chapter Two

Theories of Split-Ticket Voting

The concept of split-ticket voting is flexible enough to cover elections in both presidential and parliamentary systems, as well as to be applied to both simultaneous and non-simultaneous elections. Indeed, there are several instances where people cast more than one vote and the decision to support two different parties, or a candidate and a party that are not affiliated, can be defined as split-ticket voting. In the US, electors typically vote in a number of different contests at the same time, including those for a President and a Congressional representative. Burden and Helmke (2009) classify split-ticket voting in the US as 'vertical' or 'inter-level' split-ticket voting, given that the split occurs between elections held for offices at different levels of government. In parliamentary systems voters can engage in inter-level split-ticket voting by crossing party lines across subnational, national and supranational elections. In mixed-member electoral systems voters cast two votes to elect the same legislative chamber. In this context, Burden and Helmke (2009) talk about 'horizontal' split-ticket voting given that both votes, for the party and for the candidate, serve to elect the same legislative body. Another instance of horizontal split-ticket voting takes place under preferential systems such as Proportional Single Transferable Vote systems (PR-STV) in countries like Malta and Ireland.

Two broad theoretical viewpoints have been offered to explain patterns of vertical and horizontal split-ticket voting. The distinguishing feature between these two approaches is whether voters are believed to be voting strategically or sincerely. This chapter first reviews, briefly, the study of split-ticket voting in presidential systems and then focuses on the main theme of this book – that is split-ticket voting in parliamentary systems, and in mixed-member systems in particular. Yet, we need to start in the US, as it was there that the study of split-ticket voting was initiated.

Explanations for split-ticket voting in Presidential elections

Decades of divided government and ticket-splitting in the US led many scholars to address the question as to why some voters split their ballot by selecting a Republican for one office and a Democrat for another. Understanding divided voting behaviour is important because it contributes to divided government, a situation in which control of government institutions is shared by more than one political party. The presence of divided government has several important consequences for public policy and the representative nature of American government. Also, it is important to understand the causes of divided voting behaviour because political campaigns try to target those voters who are capable of supporting either party (Burden and Kimball 2004: 4).

Since the 1940s, analyses at the aggregate level suggested that many American voters chose a Republican President and a Democratic Congressman and vice versa (see Campbell *et al.* 1954). The lack of surveys, however, did not permit the study of the motivations behind split-ticket voting. Campbell and Miller (1957) were the first to use surveys to investigate the phenomenon. They proposed that splitters are those with a weaker partisan commitment to parties, candidates and/or issues. The data however, indicate the presence of many straight-ticket voters with no partisan attachment. This called for an additional explanation or motivation, that is to say the 'tendency toward the least effort' (Campbell and Miller 1957: 310). The authors claim that in the absence of relevant political motivation, voters cast a straight ticket, because straight voting is the easiest way for them to complete the task of voting.

After more than seventy years of research, what causes Americans to split their ticket is still open to debate (e.g., Roscoe 2003; Burden and Kimball 2004). One camp posits that US voters split intentionally to achieve a divided party government, a situation in which one party controls the executive branch and another party controls one or both houses of the Congress, the legislative branch (Alesina and Rosenthal 1995; Fiorina 1992). The opposing camp finds no support for these strategic motivations and proposes alternative explanations (Alvarez and Schousen 1993; Beck *et al.* 1992; Mattei and Howes 2000). In a nutshell, this second line of research argues that split-ticket voting can be accounted for largely by forces specific to a particular context, such as the polarisation and/or competitiveness of the district race and specific traits of competing candidates (Roscoe 2003; Maddox and Nimmo 1981; McAllister and Darcy 1992; Burden and Kimball 1998). Conversely, strategic motivations primarily derived from the policy-balancing hypothesis (Alesina and Rosenthal 1995; Fiorina 1992) have only found mixed empirical support (Beck *et al.* 1992; Mattei and Howes 2000). The policy-balancing hypothesis links to the idea that people will split their vote to achieve a specific policy outcome after the elections as they are more government-oriented than candidate-oriented (McAllister and Darcy 1992; Alvarez and Schousen 1993).

How can this conflicting evidence be reconciled? An argument, which will also prove useful in studies of vote choice under mixed systems, has been put forward by Burden and Kimball (2004: 29). The authors claim that the apparent conflicting empirical support of one theory over another may simply be an artefact derived from the reliance on different data sources. Studies using individual-level data tend to highlight that vote switching derives from voter' motivations aimed, among other things, to limiting the control exerted by a single party. Conversely, investigations utilising aggregate-level data suggest that the switching is, to a large extent, forced by the structure of the electoral competition at the district level and, in particular, by the uncompetitive nature of many congressional districts.[1]

---

1. The non-competitiveness of the US congressional elections is indeed a fact considering for instance that 'only 39 of 435 House races were won with less than 55 percent of the vote in 2012' (Garrow 2012).

In other words, existing studies using surveys find higher support for intentional split-ticket voting than studies based on aggregate data, which stress, instead, that the features of the electoral competition forces voters to behave in a specific way. So, it may well be that voters possess wishes better captured using survey data, but they can seldom act on them due to real-world constraints – evidence better captured using aggregate data and the information at the district level.[2]

In stark contrast to the vast literature on split-ticket voting in the US, the study of vote switching is scant in other presidential contexts. For instance, the study of split-ticket voting is almost completely absent from scholarship on Latin American politics, despite its centrality due to a high level of vote switching (Ames *et al.* 2009). The review of the literature on split-ticket voting in Latin America indicates a similar methodological issue found in current studies elsewhere. Recent studies based on surveys provide evidence for similar patterns of straight and split-ticket votes than the ones obtained using aggregate data, but these patterns are usually interpreted differently.

For instance, developing a micro-level theory of split-ticket voting across presidential and legislative elections in the 2000 presidential elections in Mexico, Helmke (2009) shows that voters in new democracies act as if they are choosing to divide government in line with the policy-balancing hypothesis (see also Magaloni 2004; Takahashi 2004). Despite this however, the author explains that voters' responses captured by surveys indicate that their aim is to reduce the uncertainties associated with electoral change, rather than to balance government policy outcomes. After years of single-party autocracies, Mexican voters not only strive to change the course of politics, but they also try to minimise risks associated with electing an unknown challenger candidate (Helmke 2009: 71).

Similarly, split-ticket voting in Brazil is not a consequence of policy-balancing voting according to Ames *et al.* (2009). The authors provide evidence that the over 70% rate of splitting between the presidential and congressional elections in Brazil can be explained by an institutional approach as people vote for native sons and daughters locally, whereas voting for the president is seen as a national matter. Thus, using two-city panel surveys, the authors find no support for the policy-balancing hypothesis despite the fact that aggregate results would have suggested a different conclusion.

Explanations for split-ticket voting in Parliamentary elections

Inter-level split-ticket voting – that is, voting for two different parties across levels of government, of the sort just discussed, in presidential systems – can also occur in parliamentary elections where voters may vote differently across national, local and/or supranational elections. A well-known example is at European level. The argument goes that individuals vote differently in European elections than in the

---

2. The discrepancy issue between the results provided by individual and aggregate-level data has been discussed also in other contexts (see for instance Kramer 1983). The issue will be more extensively explored in Chapter Three of this book.

general elections because the former are perceived by voters as less important, 'second-order' elections (Reif and Schmitt 1980; Reif 1984). There are two classical propositions in this context (see also Carrubba and Timpone 2005). The first one concerns the hypothesis that since European elections affect policy outcomes much less than national elections do, individuals have an incentive to use the European-wide elections as a referendum vote on national government performance. A similar argument can also be made that individuals will tend to vote more expressively at the European *elections because* their vote does not influence the formation of the government after the election (Franklin *et al.* 1995; van der Eijk and Franklin 1996).

In both cases, the predicted result is that a voter is more likely to vote for a big party in national elections and for a smaller party in the European context, because wasted voting considerations are weaker at the European level than at the national level. A wasted vote is defined as a vote cast for a party or candidate that has no chance of being elected. Evidence suggests that this is indeed the case with some significant differences in patterns of vote switching among new and old Member States (Hix and Marsh 2007; Marsh 2009). Carrubba and Timpone (2005) also test the policy-balancing hypothesis, finding mixed evidence at best. More specific findings suggest that European elections may not only be used by citizens as a referendum on the domestic performance of incumbent parties, but are also a referendum on the issue of European integration (Hobolt *et al.* 2009). The authors also find that as an upward trend on the importance of European issues is occurring, we can expect the gap between the positions of governing parties and voters on European integration to become smaller over time, as parties adopt positions closer to voters to avoid electoral punishment. This trend should ultimately reduce vote switching at the European level over time.

Another example of inter-level switching may occur across national and local elections in the same national setting, an instance of split-ticket voting that has not received much attention in the existing literature. In this regard, Rallings and Thrasher's study in Britain is a rare example of inter-level split-ticket voting in parliamentary elections. In 1979, 1997 and 2001 general and local elections in Britain coincided, so voters had to decide whether and how to distribute multiple votes across levels of government. Relying on both survey and aggregate data, the authors find that ticket-splitting is a product of both voters' attitudes and parties' strategies with contextual variables, such as the presence of incumbent candidates, playing an important role in explaining vote choice (Rallings *et al.* 1998; Rallings and Thrasher 2001, 2003).

Another contribution to inter-level switching is the work of Sanz (2008), which investigates why Spanish voters vote differently for concurrent local, regional and European elections. The author tests several mechanisms associated with second-order elections, as well as more classic explanations of split-ticket voting borrowed from the US literature, analysing both panel surveys and aggregate data. The results suggest that motivational factors weigh differently at the various electoral levels and that ideology becomes an increasingly important determinant of voting for higher levels of government.

Finally, Elklit and Kjaer (2005) use survey and aggregate data to test a 'party system' hypothesis to explain why vote switching is far more common in Denmark than in Sweden and England. Taking advantage of the fact that in all three countries national and local elections have been held simultaneously, the authors find that the differential in split-ticket voting across the three settings is due to differences in the number of parties running for elections and the discrepancy between the national and the local party systems. Specifically, split-ticket voting is far more common in Denmark than in Sweden and England. This is because the party system is different across local and national elections, providing voters with different incentives. The party-level explanation, however, leaves much variation unexplained.

Another instance of split-ticket voting in parliamentary elections concerns vote switching under preferential systems. In Ireland, Malta and Australia, voters may express preferences for as many candidates as they wish. In doing so, they are not constrained by the party labels of candidates, and voters can chose candidates within party and/or across party lines. Evidence from Ireland suggests that those voters with strong party attachments are more likely to cast a straight vote than voters with a weak attachment (Marsh 2006a). However, despite the fact that individual-level features play a critical role in explaining voting behaviour, findings indicate that the effect of system-specific voting structures on voting patterns (such as the number of district candidates each party runs and their features, primarily incumbency) should not be disregarded (Marsh and Plescia 2015).

Darcy and Marsh (1994) provide evidence that, in Australia, ballot grouping of candidates by parties encourages voters to cast more straight-ticket votes than in Ireland, where candidates are listed regardless of party affiliation. With regard to the Australian Senate, Bowler and Denemark's analysis (1993) indicate that much of voters split occurs in a strategic fashion to balance the presence of parties in the upper house. A comparative look at the Australian and US Senate supports this finding; voters in Australia engage more in strategic switching, as predicted by the policy-balancing hypothesis, than US voters do (Bean and Wattenberg 1998).

Explanations for split-ticket voting in mixed-member electoral systems

The increasing popularity of mixed systems (Carter and Farrell 2010) offers the opportunity for expanded research on this topic, assessing theories of how voters cast their ballots to fill government positions. Reasons for voters' split under mixed-member electoral systems have been the subject of scholarly investigation. Despite this, however, several methodological and substantial issues plague the understanding of split-ticket voting. Substantive issues will be identified and discussed below; methodological issues instead will be the subject of Chapter Three. This section provides a comprehensive review of the existing literature on split-ticket voting in mixed systems. It identifies the literature gaps and explains how this project is intended to fill them. I focus specifically on three main broad explanations, concerning preferences for parties and candidates, strategic and sincere voting and institutional cross-country variation. I will also focus on forced voting, discussing the issue of parties and candidates availability on the ballot paper.

Preferences for parties and candidates

The seminal finding in the US that voters with a long-term party commitment cast predominantly straight-ticket votes (Campbell and Miller 1957) has been broadly confirmed in mixed systems (e.g., Karp *et al.* 2002; Gschwend 2007; Carman and Johns 2010). However, in theory, at least, a voter could choose to vote for the same party across many offices without having any long-term party identification: indeed the voter might simply feel that parties are more important than candidates and, at a given time, one party is more attractive than all others. Deviations from straight-ticket behaviour could be expected where issues or candidate appeals might be in conflict with partisanship. This is more likely when party attachment is weak. In either case, variations in voting patterns come about because the importance of party weakens in relation to issues or candidate appeals.

There are many ways in which candidate appeal can become salient. Perhaps the most widely recognised is incumbency. This moves us away from explaining voting patterns in terms of voter characteristics and allows room for contextual factors to influence vote choice. The more incentives and opportunities there are for candidates to personalise their links with voters, the more likely it is that party and candidate appeals might conflict in the mind of the voter, whose behaviour will reflect the cross pressures that result. In New Zealand, Karp *et al.* (2002) admit that split-ticket voting in several districts may be driven by misalignment between candidate and party preferences. Burden's (2009) analysis of the 2000 election in Japan, where personal voting is rather common (e.g., Carey and Shugart 1995), suggests that candidate features matter the most in explaining the levels of split-ticket voting. And this is confirmed by Moser and Scheiner (2005: 272–274) who admit that strategic voting is potentially overestimated by the current literature because it fails to disentangle sincere split-ticket voting from strategic. This is where I turn my attention to next.

Strategic and sincere voting

Initial analyses under mixed-member electoral rules showed that at the aggregate level, small parties receive more votes in the proportional than they do in the majoritarian tier of the ballot paper. Conversely, large parties perform much better on the majoritarian than on the proportional tier (Fisher 1973). The regularity of these differences made earlier observers conclude that the wasted-vote hypothesis holds in Germany, where split-ticket voting has been most closely examined. The wasted-vote hypothesis suggests that voters may strategically desert a small party and vote for a larger alternative when the party really preferred by the voter is at risk of not being represented in parliament (e.g., Blais *et al.* 2001; 2005; Alvarez and Nagler 2000; Franklin *et al.* 1994). In mixed systems, the wasted-vote hypothesis expects that strategic voters desert a candidate on the majoritarian tier when the candidate has no chances of winning the district seat, while still supporting that party on the proportional tier.

Another argument would see voters acting strategically on the PR tier instead. Indeed, even if strategic voting is typically understood as a first-past-the-post phenomenon, scholars have suggested that strategic voting could occur also under proportional systems, especially if the district magnitude is low and the electoral threshold high (Tsebelis 1986). Threshold-insurance strategic voting has recently been gaining attention in the context of mixed systems: this second type of strategic voting occurs when supporters of large parties vote for a small party that is part of an expected coalition, to make the coalition as a whole succeed. Gschwend (2007) found that in 1998, in Germany, many supporters of the larger Christian Democratic Union (CDU)/Christian Social Union (CSU) voted strategically for the Free Democratic Party (FDP) on the PR ballot to increase the chance of a government coalition between the CDU/CSU and the FDP. Notwithstanding, only a tiny amount of voter defection from the preferred party appears to be in line with the threshold-insurance hypothesis in Germany (Pappi and Thurner 2002), New Zealand (Bowler *et al.* 2010) and Scotland (Carman and Johns 2010).

The two competing strategic hypotheses, i.e. the wasted-vote and the threshold-insurance, are both compatible with a split-ticket vote for a big party on the SMD and a small party on the PR. However, while the wasted-vote literature assumes that voters act strategically on the SMD and sincerely on the PR, the threshold-insurance literature assumes that voters act sincerely on the SMD and strategically on the PR (Shikano *et al.* 2009). There are, however, additional explanations for this observed behaviour that have received only sparse attention in the existing literature.

First, a split-ticket vote by choosing a large party on the SMD and a smaller party on the PR is compatible with sincere voting, as voters may simply like a party and a candidate that happens to run for another party (Gallagher 2001). In those few instances when attention has been given to the influence of candidates' preferences, the literature found that these indeed have a large effect on split-ticket voting (Karp *et al.* 2002; Moser and Scheiner 2005; Burden 2009). It may also simply be the case that some voters must split because their party is not running a candidate on the SMD tier of the ballot paper – a situation commonly faced by supporters of small parties. Similarly, straight-ticket voting, which is often considered a sign of sincere voting, may instead be strategic if, for instance, an adherent of a very small party that has no chance of entering parliament decides to cast a strategic straight-ticket vote for a larger party (Pappi and Thurner 2002). It is clear that the categories of straight-ticket and split-ticket voting are insufficient to distinguish between sincere and strategic voting. This book relies on a wealth of survey data and distinguishes between strategic and sincere voting based on the examination of voter preferences for both parties and candidates, rather than observed vote choice.

As a final note, Jesse (1988) was the first one to raise the point that tickets might be split for quite irrational reasons. Following this contention, Schoen (1999) found that between 1953 and 1990, no more than half of the tickets in Germany were split rationally. Some scholars have advanced suggestions that voters may be confused by the structure of the ballot paper (Cox and Schoppa 2002). These concerns, however, have not been borne out in the subsequent empirical literature in Germany and elsewhere (e.g., Bawn 1999; Karp *et al.* 2002; Karp 2006).

Institutional cross-country variation

A substantial issue considered by this book is the effect of the institutional features of the electoral system on the way people split their vote. Most mixed systems are quite unique, and different types of rules present voters with varying individual-level incentives. Also the frequency of which certain behaviours (e.g., wasted vote strategy) can be observed likely depend on the specifics of the electoral rules. Thus, while the micro-logic around sincere and strategic voting just described should be comparable across a wide range of mixed systems, nonetheless, the unique features of the system can fundamentally influence vote choice.

There are two main variants of mixed systems: 'compensatory' or mixed-proportional; 'parallel' or mixed-majoritarian; as well as a third group of systems, often defined as semi-proportional or semi-majoritarian mixed systems (Shugart and Wattenberg 2003: 12). In a mixed-proportional system, the final composition of the parliament resembles the composition obtained under pure proportional rules and the party vote is the most important determinant of the number of seats a party obtains after the election. In these systems, the two tiers are strongly linked with the PR tier, compensating for the disproportionality that may occur under majoritarian rules (Vowles 2005). Under mixed-majoritarian systems instead, no compensation exists between the two electoral tiers; under these electoral rules the candidate vote is considered the most important vote as it has a large leverage on the final composition of the parliament (Reed 2005).

Naturally, the combination of mixed rules has an impact on split-ticket voting and vote choice more generally. In the specific, scholars argue that the strong linkage between the two tiers under mixed-proportional systems encourages voters to engage in strategic voting for large candidates on the SMD, with little risk to their preferred party's success in gaining seats overall (Karp *et al.* 2002). On the other hand, under mixed-majoritarian rules, where such compensation does not exist, parties have a strong incentive to focus on winning as many single-member districts as possible, because each district seat won will add on to the national party seat total. Hence, candidates in these systems will be more likely to behave personalistically than their counterparts in compensatory systems (Moser and Scheiner 2005). Thus, overall, voters should be more likely to engage in strategic candidate voting in mixed-proportional systems than in mixed-majoritarian systems. At the same time, mixed-majoritarian systems should provide more incentives to engage in personal voting for candidates than mixed-proportional systems do.

As of today, there is a lack of comparative studies of vote choice under mixed-member electoral systems. Some comparative evidence exists but it is exclusively based on aggregate level data (see Moser and Scheiner 2005, 2009). Despite being useful in highlighting patterns and variations across countries, aggregate evidence is indirect because voter preferences for parties and candidates are not known.

To fill this gap, Chapter Four of this book investigates vote choice under nine mixed-member electoral systems: Albania, Germany, Hungary, Italy, Japan, New Zealand, Scotland, South Korea and Thailand. The analysis employs mixed-level datasets where individual-level data about voters' preferences and motivations are combined with district-level information, which takes into account the electoral context in which the vote is cast.

Forced split-ticket voting

Both sincere and strategic voting focus on voters' motivations and preferences. There is, however, a third issue to be considered, which is usually overlooked by the existing literature. Under mixed systems, the two tiers of ballot paper are not contested by the same number of parties. As a matter of fact, whereas big parties typically contest both the proportional and the majoritarian tier, small parties usually run candidates only in a few selected districts. Therefore, voters may simply be forced to split if they want to cast two votes. Forced voters are not unique to mixed systems. Using Pierce's (2003: 265) words, 'The world is full of thwarted voters'. For instance, in run-off elections vote choice is much more restricted in the second round where, usually, voters can only choose between the two best performing candidates from the first round. The literature rarely addresses the question of how people adjust to the limited party or candidate menu. This lack of knowledge is due to both data and analytical problems in measuring those voters classified as forced voters.

With regard to data-related problems, under mixed systems, if one ought to establish whether or not voters are forced, knowledge about the district in which the vote has been cast is needed; in survey data however, this information is usually not available. Even when this information is available, it remains complicated to establish whether or not the condition of forced voters is correlated with voters' willingness to split their vote. For one, forced voters have no choice but to split, which means that they cannot be included in current models in which the dependent variable measures the probability of splitting the ticket. For another, excluding all forced individuals from the analysis is problematic, because it assumes that all these voters would have cast a straight ticket if their party's candidates were available. This assumption is unrealistic though, as many voters who find their party available on both ballots split their ticket anyway. Lastly, ignoring the issue, including all voters in the analysis is problematic as well: since fewer candidates than parties run for elections, by not controlling candidate availability one risks overstating the impact sincere and strategic voting determinants have on vote choice.

To the best of my knowledge, as of today only two studies have posited attention to the issue of forced voters in the context of mixed systems. First, Benoit *et al.* (2006) offers an analysis of the 1996 national elections in Italy, where the mixed system, in use until the 2001 elections, permitted the formation of pre-electoral coalitions to be displayed on the majoritarian tier. The authors showed that Italians were more prone to split their ticket when the coalition candidate was further away, in policy terms, from the most preferred alternative on the majoritarian ballot. With regard to Johnston and Pattie (2002), the authors test how forced voters in New Zealand and Scotland reacted to the spending of parties contesting the candidate ballot. The findings suggest that, especially in Scotland, the more a party spends, the more able it is to attract forced voters on the candidate ballot, which is, by them, interpreted as an indication of strategic voting.

This book takes a difference stance on the issue and it investigates directly whether or not, and to what extent, forced voters distribute their two votes differently from non-forced voters. In particular, the issue of forced split-ticket voting is considered through two cases of study – Japan and Italy. In the first case, the availability of detailed survey data permits two kind of investigations otherwise not possible. For one, Japanese surveys contain a district-level identifier for the candidate vote allowing us to control whether or not voters find both the party and the candidate on the electoral ballot. For another, the data enable us to disentangle the individual-level rationale behind split-ticket voting given that, exceptionally, voters are asked about preferences for all parties and candidates contesting the elections, as well as being asked directly why they cast a split-ticket vote. The second case study is the Italian regional elections featuring a peculiar mixed-member electoral system where, exceptionally, pre-electoral coalitions are displayed on the ballot paper. At the same time, and differently from the national elections where pre-electoral coalitions are decided at the national level and do not vary across regions of the country, for the regional elections candidate availability varies across regions and districts, making it worthwhile to examine the extent to which the presence of specific party's candidates, as well as the overall number of candidates and parties, influence vote choice. Ultimately, by examining forced voters, this book attempts to advance the broader literature on vote choice, which rarely addresses the question of how people re-adjust to the limited electoral menu.

Summary

Free and fair elections are regarded as one of the most, if not the most, important institutions in a democracy. The importance of elections is seen through the opportunity citizens are given to pick leaders of their choice representing them in governance structures, such as parliaments. The study of how people vote in elections has occupied political scientists for decades. A peculiar but common instance of voting behaviour is split-ticket voting taking place when voters do not simply follow party line to cast the votes they have at their disposal. Split-ticket voting can be studied across various systems, presidential and parliamentary, as well as across elections within the same national context. In the different contexts, scholars have focused on disparate aspects of the phenomenon. Overall, the review of the existing literature highlights that split-ticket voting mostly reflects the interaction between individual-level features and the context in which voters cast their vote.

This chapter has provided a thorough review of the existing literature on split-ticket voting in general, and in mixed-member electoral systems in particular.

The existing literature has led to important insights into the reasons why people split their ticket and to the development of different explanations for the observed behaviour. However, when explaining ticket-splitting under mixed rules, existing studies focus most exclusively on sincere versus strategic party-centred voting. Based on the assumption that vote choice is party-centred, the literature regards straight vote and sincere voting on the one hand and split-ticket voting and strategic voting on the other hand, as almost identical. However, several alternative explanations exist that have the potential to account for observed vote choice, which deserve attention. Furthermore, the review provided in this chapter stressees that current analyses have not attempted to generalise their results across elections in the same country nor in a comparative fashion. I argue that cross-national comparison is essential since the generalisations based on one specific country experience may be inapplicable to other cases.

Hence, several unanswered questions still exist as to why and how people split their vote crossing party lines. While substantive limitations with the existing literature have been discussed in this chapter, Chapter Three deals with methodological issues pertaining to the measurement of vote choice under mixed rules.

Measuring Split-Ticket Voting

This chapter deals exclusively with the measurement of the dependent variable: split-ticket voting. The study of how people vote has a fundamental individual-level component because it reflects a choice based on voter preferences and motivations. At the same time, voting can be conceived as an aggregate-level phenomenon influenced by the context in which votes are being cast, e.g., the number of candidates available on the ballot paper, the competitiveness of the electoral race and so forth. Aggregate and individual-level data permit the study of different dimensions of split-ticket voting. Each type of data are, however, plagued by several methodological flaws. I review these limitations in this chapter and point to improvements on the use of both types of data to study split-ticket voting.

To this end, this chapter first reviews current approaches for the measurement of split-ticket voting, then identifies gaps and limitations and, finally, it proposes alternative approaches. It needs to be emphasised at the outset that this chapter is not intended to settle on a perfect set of data or model, but rather aims to highlight weaknesses and strengths of existing measurements. Substantive analyses in following chapters of this book build on the methodological findings and methods discussed in this chapter.

Individual-level data

For the most part, existing analyses of split-ticket voting have been using post-electoral surveys which represent the unique access point to voters' preferences and motivations.

Common approach

Surveys usually ask respondents about their party and their candidate vote using two separate questions. With regard to the party vote, respondents are normally asked: 'For which *party* have you voted for on the proportional part of the ballot paper?' Similarly, for the candidate vote they are asked: 'For which *candidate* have you voted for on the majoritarian part of the ballot paper?'. The classical dependent variable in studies of vote choice under mixed systems is a dummy variable which takes a value of 0 when voters choose a party and the affiliated candidate and 1 otherwise (e.g., Schoen 1999; Cox and Schoppa 2002; Carman and Johns 2010). A few subsequent studies have differentiated the category of splitters into separate groups. In the specific, Gschwend (2007) differentiate those casting a 'supposedly strategic' split (i.e. choosing a small party on the proportional, and a large party on the majoritarian, tier) from all other splitters defined as 'supposedly non-strategic'.

Karp *et al.* (2002) instead focus only on split-ticket voting between ideologically close parties, as the rest is considered by the authors as mostly random. The existing literature has then focused on two main incentives to cast a split-ticket vote. The first is a strategic candidate vote to avoid wasting a vote on the majoritarian tier while still supporting the most preferred party on the proportional tier. The second is a strategic party vote on the proportional tier to favour the formation a specific coalition outcome, also referred to as a threshold-insurance vote.

The concepts of strategic candidate and strategic party votes under mixed rules postulate that 'party preference is the yardstick for both the first and second vote' (Pappi and Thurner 2002: 214). Hence, split-ticket voting is commonly used as a measure of strategic voting, as voters who split their vote are assumed to express their true party preference in one tier but vote strategically on the other. However, the assumption of strategic voting among splitters, as well as the assumption of sincere voting among straight voters, may be very problematic. Several scholars have raised concerns regarding the approach that uses the categories of straight and split-ticket voting to study voting behaviour under mixed rules (see for instance the discussion in Schoen (1999: 482–484) and Pappi and Thurner (2002: 212–215)). However, limited data have until now meant that sincere and strategic voting could only be studied by means of observed behaviour. Specifically, survey respondents were only asked to rate the parties and their chances to obtain seats, while no analogous questions were asked about the candidates. As discussed by Herrmann and Pappi (2008: 233) this fact compelled scholars to assume that voter support for various candidates was guided exclusively by party preferences.

Below, I will first explain that in mixed systems, straight-vote is not synonymous with sincere voting and split-ticket voting is not synonymous with strategic voting. I then discuss the need of alternative measurements for the dependent and independent variables in studies of vote choice under mixed rules. In the context of this book, 'sincere vote' describes a situation in which the voter chooses the most preferred option (i.e., party or candidate) from a menu of alternatives. Given that on the proportional tier, citizens vote for parties and on the majoritarian tier they vote for candidates, I define the vote as sincere when the voter simultaneously chooses the most preferred party and the most preferred candidate. The term 'sincere only on the PR' means that the voter chooses the most preferred party on the proportional tier but not the most preferred candidate on the majoritarian tier; 'sincere only on the SMD' means that the voter chooses the most preferred candidate but not the most preferred party and, finally, 'non-sincere' indicates that the voter is neither picking the most preferred party nor the most preferred candidate. Note that voting against sincere preferences is not automatically regarded as strategic in the context of this book. Indeed, I speak about non-sincere vote rather than strategic vote when voters are not picking parties and candidates in line with their preferences. This decision is based on the fact that voting against sincere preferences is not a sufficient condition to define vote choice as strategic. Another condition must be met: the vote is strategic not when voters deviate from sincere preferences but when they do so to influence the election outcome (e.g., Fisher 2004; Blais *et al.* 2006).

Now, consider a hypothetical constituency contested by two parties (A and B), each nominating 1 candidate (A and B) as shown in Table 3.1. For the sake of the example, let us assume that Party A is a large party while party B is a small party. Current studies measure sincere and strategic voting from observed patterns of vote choice. Hence, in line with the existing literature, Voter 1 would cast a straight sincere vote; Voter 2 is a case of strategic split and, finally, Voter 3 is a case of non-strategic split. Let us see what happens when one considers simultaneously observed vote choice and true voter preferences.

Starting with an observed straight vote, Voter 1 can only be considered sincere when the voter actually favours the candidate affiliated with their most preferred party (Voter 1a); the remaining are cases of non-sincere straight vote. First, categories b and c of Voter 1 represent voters who have separate preferences

Table 3.1: Straight and split-ticket voting when considering vote and preferences simultaneously: a hypothetical case of three voters and two parties, a larger party A and a smaller party B, each nominating a candidate.

Voter	PR ballot		SMD ballot		Voting patterns		
	Vote choice	*Prefs*	*Vote choice*	*Prefs*	*Observed*	*Electoral calculus*	*Real vote choice*
1	Party A		Cand A		Straight	Sincere	
a		Party A		Cand A			Sincere
b		Party A		Cand B			Sincere only on PR
c		Party B		Cand A			Sincere only on SMD
d		Party B		Cand B			Non- sincere
2	Party B		Cand A		Split	Strategic	Strategic
a		Party A		Cand A			Sincere only on SMD
b		Party A		Cand B			Non-sincere
c		Party B		Cand A			Sincere
d		Party B		Cand B			Sincere only on PR
3	Party A		Cand B		Split	Non-Strategic	
a		Party A		Cand A			Sincere only on PR
b		Party A		Cand B			Sincere
c		Party B		Cand A			Non-sincere
d		Party B		Cand B			Sincere only on SMD

for parties and candidates but decide to cast a straight-ticket vote for either their most preferred party or their most preferred candidate's party. Voter 1b may well recognise that their preferred local candidate, Candidate B, has no chance of winning the majoritarian race and thus they decide to cast a straight vote for the larger Party A. Voter 1c may start by choosing a majoritarian candidate and follow the candidate to a party with their proportional vote. It is fair to assume that in countries where local candidates matter even more than parties, like in Japan, for instance (Reed 2003; Burden 2009), Voter 1c may not represent a minority. Only by having full access to true voters' preferences are we able to recognise that Voter 1b is casting a sincere vote only on the PR, whereas Voter 1c casts a sincere vote on the SMD only. Conversely, having access exclusively to preferences for parties may lead to classify both Voters 1b and 1c in the same category of sincere straight voters. In countries where rich individual-level data exists, I find about 6 per cent of Voter 1b in New Zealand and 8 per cent in Japan and Germany, and at least an equal size of Voter 1c across all countries.[1] Straight votes can also be completely non-sincere when, for instance, supporters of a (very) small party decide to vote for a larger alternative on both tiers of the ballot paper (Voter 1d). To give an idea, in the countries under scrutiny in this book I find that a little more than 2 per cent of voters across all countries can be classified as Voter 1d.

Moving to split-ticket voting, Voter 2 chooses a small party on the PR and a big party on the SMD. This vote would be classified by the existing literature as strategic split given that it conforms simultaneously to a strategic candidate and/or strategic party vote. Conversely, Voter 3 is an example of a random split-ticket vote since the vote for the small party's Candidate B on the SMD may be regarded as wasted. Yet again, knowledge of the true party and candidate preferences would enable us to capture that, at least part of the strategic split (Voter 2) and of the non-strategic split (Voter 3), may simply be due to sincere voting. This applies to all cases where voters favour a candidate not affiliated with the most preferred party (Voter 2c and Voter 3b). There are about 10 per cent of Voter 2b in New Zealand, roughly 2 per cent in Germany and 5 per cent in Japan. I also find about 8 per cent of Voter 3c in New Zealand and roughly 4 per cent in Germany and Japan.

In addition, by having access only to party preferences, one is unable to distinguish voters in the category labelled here as sincere only on the PR (Voter 2d) from voters being sincere only on the SMD (Voter 2a). Finally, it seems harder to explain the motivations behind Voter 2b and Voter 3c, both defined in Table 3.1 as non-sincere. They might result from protest voting or simply a

---

1. Of all mixed systems that have extant public opinion surveys, the 2002 New Zealand Election Study (http://www.nzes.org/exec/show/2002, accessed July 2014), the 2009 German Election Study (GESIS Data Archive, doi: 10.4232/1.11373) and the 2003 Japanese Election Study (JES III Project Team, University of Tokyo, available at http://ssjda.iss.u-tokyo.ac.jp/en/access/how/, accessed July 2014) are, to the best of my knowledge, the few ones that include a pre-electoral wave that asks voters a number of key questions about expectations of the electoral outcome and preferences for both candidates and parties. I thus use these data here to provide some evidence about the patterns of sincere and strategic voting shown in Table 3.1. Data availability is further discussed in Chapter Four.

misunderstanding of the electoral rules. In any case one is unable to explain these behaviours unless additional information on voters' features, such as political knowledge, is made available. I find very low levels of these voters across all countries (below 1 per cent).

To sum up, this example shows that, potentially, current analyses of split-ticket voting might be underestimating strategic voting because strategic voters can be found also among straight voters. At the same time, the literature likely overestimates strategic split-ticket voting since split-ticket voting can simply be a result of voters voting for candidates rather than for parties. Classifying sincere and strategic voting from observed behaviour may result in a severely limited view of vote choice in mixed systems. Specifically, not accounting for the empirical presence of alternative sincere voting motivations entails measurement error in the actual identification of both sincere and strategic voters.

An alternative approach

Given that one cannot infer about sincere and strategic voting simply observing at the individual-level whether or not a voter split their vote, subsequent analyses presented in this book rely on different strategies to study vote choice. The first strategy is to analyse the two votes (the party and the candidate vote) separately rather than in conjunction, as is the practice in the existing literature. The second strategy, pursued in this book, is to use the classical dependent variable but to alter the measurement of the independent variables.

For the first strategy, in the initial step I compare the pre-electoral voting intentions to actual vote choice in the two parts of the electoral ballot. The broad idea is that since the two votes are cast by the same voter during the same election, there should be no major differences across the two votes when it comes to the comparison of intended and actual vote. In other words, there is no reason to expect a priori that intentions and actual vote should be more similar in one tier of the ballot paper when compared to the other. If voters are found to behave differently in two tiers across the pre- and post-electoral settings, I will examine why by considering sincere and strategic voting incentives. In a second step, I use actual vote choice as a dependent variable. Hence, the dependent variable does not measure whether voters cast a split rather than a straight vote, but rather the attention is given to what explains vote choice in two parts of the electoral ballot separately. The aim is to assess what explains the two votes and whether or not there are substantial differences when it comes to the influence of sincere, strategic and institutional factors. The same set of variables is applied across countries and across votes.

In a second strategy, I follow the standard approach to the study of split-ticket voting by building a dummy taking a value of 0 every time the respondent casts a straight vote and 1 otherwise. However, all independent variables are not measured considering the party voted for exclusively, as is usually done in the existing literature, but by taking into account the candidate voted for as well. For instance, in standard multivariate models of split-ticket voting, the party identification variable takes a value of 1 if the respondent identifies with the party voted for on the proportional tier and 0 otherwise. In this book, this classical measure is compared with a candidate-centred measure whereby the party identification variable takes a value of 1 if the respondent identifies with the party of the candidate supported on the majoritarian tier and 0 otherwise. And so forth for all independent variables. The comparison of the two models, one party-centred and one candidate-centred, allows us to check whether or not voters consider the two votes similarly and to examine to extent to which specific operationalisation of the independent variables affects substantive conclusions on vote choice.

Ultimately, these two strategies of analysis, i.e., looking at the two votes separately rather than in conjunction and altering the operationalisation of the independent variables, enable me to reason about sincere and strategic voting avoiding the limitations of more classical approaches. Furthermore, these innovative strategies permit us to shed light on the issue of forced split-ticket voting and to compare the behaviour of forced and non-forced voters to assess whether or not they cast their two votes differently. This represents an important innovation since forced voters are largely overlooked by the existing literature, as already mentioned in Chapter Two. This book however, does not focus only on individual-level data but also leverages on aggregate electoral results; why and how this is done is explained next.

Aggregate-level data

Surveys represent the only access point to individual-level motivations and they allow us to explore differences in the characteristics of voters. Nonetheless, surveys suffer from a number of limitations, some of which are particularly relevant to the analysis conducted in this book. Firstly, surveys suffer from respondent bias. This issue has been discussed extensively in the US where the study of split-ticket voting began (e.g., Wright 1990; Burden and Kimball 2004). In mixed-member electoral systems similar problems have been encountered. For instance, in the Scottish case Carman and Johns (2010: 386) found sampling and response biases that are not corrected by the population weight, with regard to overstated straight votes for small parties.

A second disadvantage of survey data relates to this book's aim to investigate split-ticket voting variation, not just between countries, but from within, district to district. Survey data are simply not up to the task given that they do not often provide information that is representative of all the districts inside a country (Gschwend et al. 2003; Johnston and Pattie 2003). Another drawback has been discussed by Benoit et al. (2006) and it concerns the difficultly of linking survey data to demographic information at the district unit. Such limitation is due to the fact that surveys usually do not contain information about the district in which the two votes have been cast. Linking vote choice to the features of the district-level electoral competition is of uttermost importance for the study of strategic voting since it is precisely these features that largely determine the incentives to cast a strategic vote (see Niemi et al. (1992) among others). The impossibility of linking survey data to the voting district complicates the analysis conducted in this book and, generally speaking, it limits comprehensive analyses of voting behaviour. Due to these limitations, this book also employs aggregate electoral results.

Aggregate data has the advantage of dealing with how people actually voted, rather than how they said they voted (Bernhagen and Marsh 2010: 460). Aggregate data also enable a focus on the parties' strategic actions, such as the decision to run a candidate on specific SMD contexts, and, hence, the impact they have on split-ticket voting. Moreover, aggregate data allow the analysis of split-ticket voting at the district level, investigating where and when split-ticket voting is more common. Despite these positive notes however, the use of aggregate data for the study of split-ticket voting is plagued by methodological flaws. Importantly, because aggregate data only reports the total party and candidate vote, any inference of electoral behaviour at the aggregate level is limited by the well-known 'ecological fallacy' problem as discussed next.

Common approach

In Table 3.2, also known as 'RxC contingency table', row (R) entries represent the votes gained by parties, whereas the values in the columns (C) represent the votes obtained by candidates. In the case of each geographical unit we know how many individuals cast a vote for a specific party and for a certain candidate. However, due to the secrecy of the ballot paper, we do not have information on how many individuals voted simultaneously for a specific party *and* a certain candidate. In other words, for each electoral unit i, the marginals T_A^i, T_B^i, T_C^i and X_A^i, X_B^i, X_C^i of the contingency table are known while all the β_{rc}^i need to be estimated. The task of filling in a contingency table from information about its margins is known as 'ecological inference'.

When relying on aggregate data, the existing literature uses the net measure of split-ticket voting, calculating the difference between the votes gained by the party and the affiliated candidate in a certain district, i.e., the difference between the rows and columns in Table 3.2. Current studies then normally use Ordinary Least Squares regression (OLS) to regress the net measure of ticket-splitting on

Table 3.2: Ecological inference for straight and split-ticket voting

Party vote	Candidate vote				
	Candidate A	*Candidate B*	*Candidate C*	*Other(s)*	
Party A	β_{AA}^i	β_{AB}^i	β_{AC}^i	$1-\sum^c \beta_{Ac}^i$	X_A^i
Party B	β_{BA}^i	β_{BB}^i	β_{BC}^i	$1-\sum^c \beta_{Bc}^i$	X_B^i
Party C	β_{CA}^i	β_{CB}^i	β_{CC}^i	$1-\sum^c \beta_{Cc}^i$	X_C^i
	T_A^i	T_B^i	T_C^i	$1-\sum^c \beta_C^i$	

a number of factors, such as incumbency, competitiveness of the district race and so forth (e.g., Bawn 1999; Kostadinova 2002; Moser and Scheiner 2005). This measure of the dependent variable is flawed by significant problems as it only provides the minimum level of split-ticket voting that actually takes place and it is not able to account for all the cross-voting among parties and candidates (Cowart 1974; King 1997). One possible solution to this problem is to use indirect methods able to provide estimates of split-ticket voting.

Several methods have been proposed for the estimation of RxC tables of the sort shown in Table 3.2. (e.g., King *et al.* [2004], De Sio [2003], Park *et al.* [2014] and Elff *et al.* [2008]). In this chapter, I focus exclusively on two of these methods: the Rosen *et al.* (2001) and the Greiner and Quinn (2009). My exclusive focus on these two methods is based on several reasons. First, when compared to other methods such as the Elff *et al.* (2008), the Rosen *et al.* (2001) and the Greiner and Quinn (2009) rely exclusively on aggregate-level data; on the contrary, the Elff *et al.* (2008) method requires an estimation of a general transition matrix which uses individual-level data (see also Johnston and Pattie 2000; 2004), which, in cases like the Italian regional elections, and more recent elections in Japan under scrutiny in this book, are not available. Second, compared to other estimation methods, the Rosen *et al.* (2001) and the Greiner and Quinn (2009) methods are straightforwardly implemented using in-build packages in R. Given that these methods are ready available, a test of their performance can serve other scholars facing the issue of how to estimate cells of complex contingency tables. Not least, both methods allow a series of important extensions, e.g. use of covariates and specification of the priors, not usually available for other methods. (Appendix 3.II considers these extensions in more details; Appendix 3.I discusses earlier methods of estimation).

The Rosen et al. (2001) method

Rosen and his co-authors propose two approaches for the estimation of RxC tables. The Bayesian approach extends the binomial-beta hierarchical model developed by King *et al.* (1999) which was only applicable to tables with two rows and two columns (2x2 tables). This model itself builds upon the seminal work of King (1997). Referring to Table 3.2, in the first stage, the Rosen *et al.* (2001) method assumes that the stochastic component $T_c^i, = (T_A^i, T_B^i T_C^i)$ follows a Multinomial distribution with systematic component $\Theta = \sum_r^r \beta_{rc}^i X_r^i$ where $r = A, B, C$ and $c = A, B, C$. On the second level of this hierarchical model, the stochastic component $\beta_{rc}^i = (\beta_{AA}^i, \beta_{BA}^i, ..., \beta_{rc}^i)$ follows a Dirichlet distribution with systematic component

$$\alpha_{rc}^i = \frac{d_r \exp(\gamma_{rc} + \delta_{rc} Z_j)}{d_r(1 + \sum_{j=1}^{C-1} \exp(\gamma_{rj} + \delta_{rj} Z_i))} = \frac{\exp(\gamma_{rc} + \delta_{rc} Z_i)}{1 + \sum_{j=1}^{C-1} \exp(\gamma_{rj} + \delta_{rj} Z_j)}.$$

In the third and final stage, the model assumes that the regression parameters (the γ_{rc}^i and the δ_{rc}^i) are a priori independent with a flat prior. The parameters d_r, $r = 1,...,R$, are assumed to follow exponential distributions with mean $1/\lambda$ (Rosen *et al.* 2001:137–138). The marginals of the posterior distribution are obtained using Gibbs sampler (Tanner 1996). As in the 2x2 case, the inferential procedure employs Markov chain Monte Carlo (MCMC) methods. As explained by Rosen *et al.* (2001) their approach can be computationally quite intense and for complex models the assessment of convergence may not be straightforward. They thus propose a simpler non-linear, least-squares approach (hereafter referred to as Ecological Inference- Multinomial Dirichlet method or EI-MD) which is a direct approximation of their MCMC method but based on first moments rather than on the entire likelihood. As such, it provides quicker inference via nonlinear least-squares.

The Greiner and Quinn (2009) method

The second method I explore below has been proposed by Greiner and Quinn (2009) (hereafter referred to as Ecological Inference-Multinomial Logistic method or EI-ML). For each contingency table of the sort shown in Table 3.2, the rows are assumed to follow mutually independent multinomials, conditional on separate probability vectors, which are denoted by Θ_r for $r = 1$ to R (R being the number of rows in each contingency table). Each Θ_r then undergoes a multidimensional logistic transformation, using the last (right-most) column as the reference category.[2] This results in R transformed vectors of length C; these transformed vectors are stacked to form a single ω vector corresponding to that contingency table. The omega vectors are assumed to follow (*i.i.d.*) a multivariate normal distribution (see Greiner and Quinn [2009: 70–72]). This method is structurally similar to the Rosen *et al.* (2001), although within-row relationships appear to be less constrained in the Greiner and Quinn (2009) as this model uses the stacked additive logistic normal distribution instead of mutually independent Dirichlet distributions.

Tests on alternative approaches

As of today, almost no empirical evaluations have characterised the Rosen *et al.* (2001) and the Greiner and Quinn (2009). The sections below evaluate the accuracy of these recent models, today straightforwardly implemented using the free software environment R, to decide which one to employ in substantive analysis of split-ticket voting.[3]

---

2. In their article Greiner and Quinn (2009:70) choose the 'abstain' column as reference category. In the results presented below I use as reference a residual category representing the sum of party vote cast for parties receiving less than 2 per cent of the vote but it is important to stress that changing this reference category did not alter the results significantly.

3. Specifically, to apply the EI-MD method I use the code integrated into *Zelig* (version 3.5.1), which implements models using a nonlinear least squares approximation (Wittenberg *et al.* 2007). As of June 2015 the same model is available through the R package *eiPack* (http://cran.r-project.org/web/packages/eiPack/index.html, accessed July 2014). Using either of these packages provide substantively identical results but the *eiPack* package contains additional features than its older counterpart. The EI-ML, is implemented using the tune function in the *RxCEcolInf* package in R available at http://cran.r-project.org/web/packages/RxCEcolInf/index.html (accessed July 2014) (Greiner *et al.* 2013).

To examine the performance of the two estimation methods I collected electoral data from New Zealand and Scotland at the lowest levels of aggregation for which electoral data are made available– that is the polling station level. In particular, I have data from about 5,000 polling stations per each year of election. Given that I examine voting patterns for three years of election for New Zealand (2002, 2005 and 2008) and one year for Scotland (2007) I deal with at least 20,000 ecological units. There are several reasons why I use these data and these two contexts. First and foremost, for these two contexts I dispose exceptionally of the *true* quantities of interest.[4] Indeed due to the secrecy of the ballot paper, patterns of split- and straight-ticket voting are not normally available to researchers which as per Table 3.2 can only access the combined party and candidate vote (that is only the marginal of the table are known). In both countries however, I know exactly for each district how many people cast a straight and a split-ticket vote for each party and candidate running for elections that is also the internal cells of Table 3.2 are known. This extraordinary opportunity of knowing the true quantities of interest guarantees the accuracy of the empirical tests.

Second, the two countries exhibit conspicuous variation between and within districts (also known as *electorate* in New Zealand and *constituency* in Scotland), which is of great importance for the evaluation of the conditions under which the two methods perform better. Specifically, the variation between districts in each country affects the size and the values of the contingency tables to be estimated. Starting with the size, while the number of parties, i.e. the rows of our contingency tables, is constant across districts in any given election, the number of candidates, i.e. the columns, varies across districts in any given election: in Scotland, the number of candidates ranges between four and seven; in New Zealand, the number ranged between four and eleven in 2002; between three and fourteen in 2005 and between two and fourteen in 2008. Ten parties contested the 2007 election in Scotland but fourteen in 2002; and nineteen in 2005 and 2008 in New Zealand. This variation provides me with contingency tables as small as 10X4, in Scotland, to as large as 19X14 in New Zealand.

When it comes to the marginals of the contingency tables, the party (X_A, X_B, X_C) and the candidate vote (T_A, T_B, T_C) vary considerably across districts. For instance in 2008, the Labour party in New Zealand received a maximum amount of vote of 66.5 per cent in the district of Hauraki and a minimum of 19 per cent in Hunua. Smaller parties face similar variation, for instance still in 2008, the New Zealand First party vote ranged from as low as 1.5 per cent in Wellington Central to as high as 10.4 per cent in Tauranga. Concerning the internal values of the tables, Figure 3.1 provides an idea of the variation to be estimated. Figure 3.1 shows the true percentages of straight-ticket voting (on the total of the party vote)

---

4. The Electoral Commission in New Zealand continues to make this data available on its website (www.electionresults.org.nz) while for Scotland data were only available, exceptionally, for the 2007 election (www.scotlandoffice.gov.uk/scotlandoffice). (accessed July 2014)

Figure 3.1: Party-level true percentage of straight vote at the district level, %

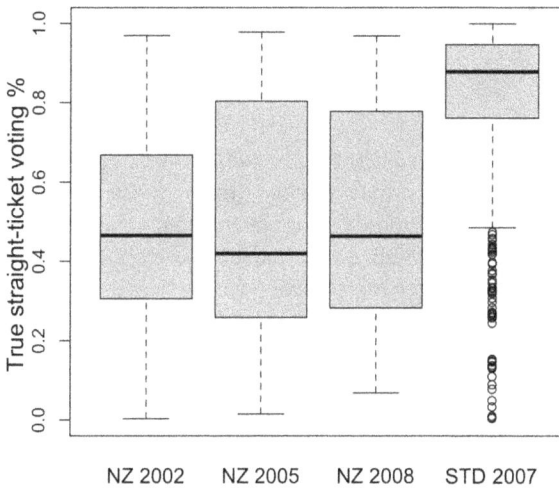

Notes: The plot displays the true percentage of straight-ticket voting received by each party at the district level. Only parties that run on both electoral tiers are included in the plot. NZ refers to New Zealand and STD to Scotland.

Source: own elaboration from data available at www.electionresults.org.nz/ for New Zealand and at www.scotlandoffice.gov.uk/ for Scotland. (accessed 3 July 2014)

received by each party at the district level for each year of election considered in this chapter. Levels of straight-ticket voting are much lower in New Zealand compared with Scotland where the distribution is skewed to the left. The shape in New Zealand is due to the presence of the two big parties (the Labour and the National parties) receiving high levels of straight-ticket voting, and a large group of smaller parties, such as the Greens and the New Zealand First (NZF), receiving far lower percentages of straight-ticket voting. In the case of Scotland, smaller parties do not usually contest the candidate vote and thus the majority of observations in Figure 3.1 concern the Labour, Conservative, Liberal Democrats (Lib Dem) and the Scottish National Party (SNP), which generally receive high percentages of straight-ticket voting.

There is also another variation that is mostly relevant to assess the performance of the two methods and it is related to the within-district variation. I refer here to both the number of aggregate units across which the district-level parameters need to be estimated as well as the across-unit variance. Since ecological inference is essentially a problem of aggregation, examining circumstances when this sort of homogeneity is not present across the aggregate units is highly important (Park *et al.* 2014). When it comes to the number of aggregate units across which the district-level parameters need to be estimated, the number of polling stations in New Zealand ranges from 113–24 with the five Maori districts featuring almost

650 polling stations.[5] Similarly for Scotland, the number of polling stations ranges from 103–22. When it comes to the across unit variance, I take into account how dissimilar the polling stations inside a specific district are and I examine whether this dissimilarity affects the overall estimates.

Empirical evidence

For both estimation methods I first ran simulations for all parties as separate rows and for all candidates as separate columns. I then ran a second set of simulations by collapsing rows and columns for parties and candidates obtaining less than 2 per cent of the total vote, which I call 'reduced forms'. Given the large number of parties contesting the elections and considering the computational intensity of the two methods, reducing rows and columns may save a large amount of time during the estimation. It is thus worth investigating whether and how reducing the dimension of tables affects the results.

Observed estimates

To appreciate the performance of the EI-MD and EI-ML methods, the comparison between estimated and true values is provided by party at the district level, thus looking at the β_{rc}^i as provided by the two methods directly. Figure 3.2 illustrates party percentages of true straight-ticket vote in each district plotted against the corresponding estimated quantities. The closer the dots are to the diagonal line, the better the method performs and the more similar the estimated quantities are to the true values. The EI-MD method tends to be quite precise in the estimation of values of interest; for bigger parties it tends to overestimate straight-ticket voting while in most of the cases the EI-MD underestimates the straight vote for smaller parties. Without fail, the EI-ML method performs the worst as it consistently overestimates straight vote values in the majority of cases. Generally speaking, both methods perform better in the case of Scotland than in that of New Zealand.

There are a few point estimates that exhibit extraordinary large errors. Most of them represent tiny parties. There are, however, a few outliers illustrating observations for big parties as shown in Figure 3.2. I examine these point estimates further and notice that they most often represent observations from the Maori districts in New Zealand. These seven districts feature peculiar electoral competitions that translate into contingency tables characterised by high values in the row marginals but low values in the corresponding column marginal for big parties; the reverse situation

---

5. Maori electorates are Ikaroa-Rawhiti, Tainui, Tamaki Makaurau, TeTai Hauauru, Te Tai Tokerau, Te Tai Tonga and Waiariki. These seven districts in New Zealand are characterised by a larger maximum number of polling stations that is 645 in 2002, 691 in 2005 and 680 in 2008 election.

6. The Maori districts are characterised by the same number of rows, i.e. parties, as the other districts but by far fewer columns, i.e. candidates, as only the Maori party and, as a rule, one or both the Labour and National parties run candidates; second, the two big parties, still receive relatively large share of party vote in these districts as compared to the other parties, even though their candidates perform poorly while local Maori candidates perform rather well.

Figure 3.2: Estimated (EI-MD and EI-ML) versus true straight-ticket voting by party, %

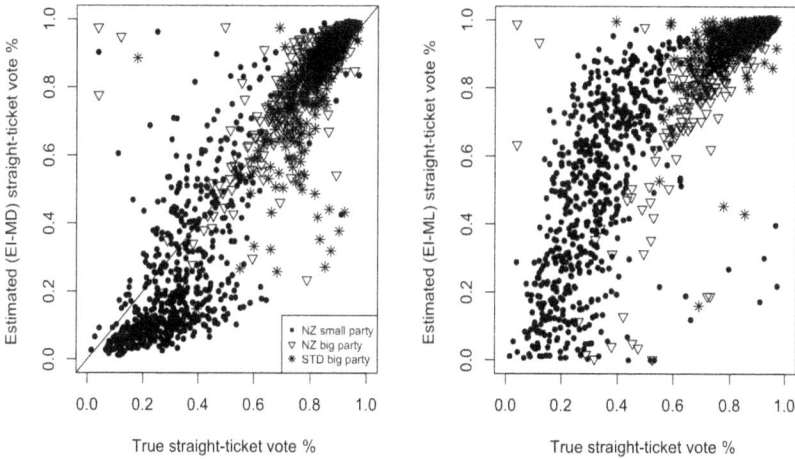

Notes: Each dot represents the amount of straight-ticket votes received by each party in a certain district. The plots only include parties that also run a candidate on the SMD tier of the ballot paper. Big parties in New Zealand are the Labour and National parties; in Scotland big parties are the Conservative, the Labour, the Scottish National Party and the Liberal Democrats. Small parties in New Zealand include the Greens, the ACT and the NZF; small parties in Scotland are not included since they did not run candidates.

is true for the Maori party.[6] In these cases, both methods significantly overestimate straight-ticket voting for large parties and significantly underestimate values for the Maori party. The regularity of these outliers suggests that the ecological results will probably miss the mark when rows and corresponding columns are characterised by extremely non-homogenous values – as is the case for the Maori districts.

The error in the estimates

Moving to the error in the estimates, I start by analysing how much the results miss the mark. To statically evaluate the error in the estimates I follow Liu (2007: 16) and use the Root Mean Squared Error (Root-MSE) using the formula:

$$RMSE = \sqrt{mean(\beta^{estimated} - \beta^{true})^2}$$

Root-MSE measures the differences between the estimated and the true observed values and enables us to assess both the accuracy of the point estimates (i.e. how biased the estimator is) and the efficiency of point estimators. Root-MSE ranges from 0 to 1 with '0' meaning that the estimated values are identical to the true values; conversely, larger values of Root-MSE indicate less precise estimates. Table 3.3 shows the values of Root-MSE by party across years of election. The EI-ML method results without collapsing columns are not shown in Table 3.3 as it

Table 3.3: Root–MSE: party level straight-ticket voting at the district level, by election

	EI-MD	EI-MD reduced	EI-ML	EI-ML reduced	N
2002 New Zealand					
All parties	0.1590	*0.1539*		0.1997	273
Labour	0.1655	*0.1280*	–	0.1641	69
National	0.1419	*0.1235*	–	0.1538	69
Greens	0.1547	*0.1478*	–	0.2644	56
ACT	0.1582	*0.1510*	–	0.1829	23
NZF	0.1368	*0.2357*	–	0.2253	56
2005 New Zealand					
All parties	0.1679	*0.1665*		0.2549	275
Labour	0.0777	*0.0878*	–	0.1573	69
National	0.0937	*0.0941*	–	0.0897	62
Greens	0.1560	*0.1773*	–	0.3606	55
ACT	0.1528	*0.1351*	–	0.3224	38
NZF	0.1794	*0.1886*	–	0.2323	51
2008 New Zealand					
All parties	0.1463	*0.1377*		0.2373	264
Labour	0.0838	*0.0766*	–	0.1259	70
National	0.1418	*0.1412*	–	0.1530	63
Greens	0.1741	*0.1607*	–	0.3273	58
ACT	0.1118	*0.1036*	–	0.2669	13
NZF	0.2184	*0.2048*	–	0.2394	60
2007 Scotland					
All parties	0.1437	*0.1193*		0.1724	288
Labour	0.1838	*0.1279*	–	0.1591	72
Conservative	0.1387	*0.1191*	–	0.1448	72
Lib Dems	0.1537	*0.1421*	–	0.2187	72
SNP	0.0789	*0.0785*	–	0.1569	72

Notes: Root-MSE is calculated using the formula: $RMSE = \sqrt{mean(\beta^{estimated} - \beta^{true})^2}$ where β_{rc} is the amount of straight-ticket vote received by each party in a district. Reduced form results are those obtained collapsing rows and columns for parties receiving less than 2 per cent of the total vote. Calculations include only parties that run also a candidate. *Key to party:* NZF-New Zealand First; ACT-Association of Consumers and Taxpayers; Lib Dem – Liberal Democrats; SNP-Scottish National Party. Italics indicate the best performing method. N refers to the number of observations for the Root-MSE calculation.

was not feasible to estimate quantities of interest for all districts in a specific year of election. In other words, the EI-ML takes much longer to provide estimates than the EI-MD method and the technique fails to provide quantities of interest (i.e. it fails to reach convergence) when the estimation tables have a number of rows and/ or columns that exceed 15. Consequently, the reduction of the number of rows and/or columns is not only appealing because it saves time but it is also necessary in the case of the EI-ML method. Nevertheless, as it is the case for the EI-MD method, the quantities in those few cases where the estimates were obtained did not show major variations before and after collapsing columns.

To ease the comparison across reduced and non-reduced forms, in the calculation of the Root-MSE I only include straight-ticket voting levels for the parties where rows and columns have been estimated separately; in other words, for the calculations of the Root-MSE for the full form of the EI-MD I do not include estimates for very small parties and for the reduced form of the EI-MD and EI-ML I do not include the 'other' category, which represents the sum of all tiny parties. Overall values of Root-MSE are pretty low for both estimation methods. For each row, the table shows the estimator that performs best in italics: it is straightforward to see that the EI-MD in its reduced form provides the most accurate results. In addition, it appears that the error is smaller for big parties than for small parties.

Estimates, sample and variation

To perform more rigorous tests I calculate the difference between the true proportion of straight-ticket vote (estimand) and estimated proportion from the aggregate precinct data (realised estimate). Because the procedure calculates these differences for each individual cell, I do not have space to present all these results for a single year of election, let alone for the four elections discussed in this chapter. Instead I focus on specific features of the unit of aggregation that are directly linked to concerns common to all estimators: 1. concerns related to the estimation of the values of interest when the sample size is small, i.e. number of polling stations by district, and 2. concerns related to the performance of the estimator when there is substantial diversity across the polling stations within each district.

Figure 3.3 shows the differences by number of polling stations; the panel on the left shows these calculations for the EI-MD while the panel on the right shows these calculations for the EI-ML. First, Figure 3.3 shows that the variance in the distribution decreases as the sample size increases. There is, however, a big difference between the values for big and small parties where the former are much more precise. Overall though, the bias remains close to the absolute value of 0.2. Figure 3.4 shows differences by number of rows and columns; it shows that as this number increases so does the variance in the error distribution. There is a confirmation however, that the error is mostly associated with the estimates for small parties.

Figure 3.3: Difference between estimate and estimand, by number of polling stations

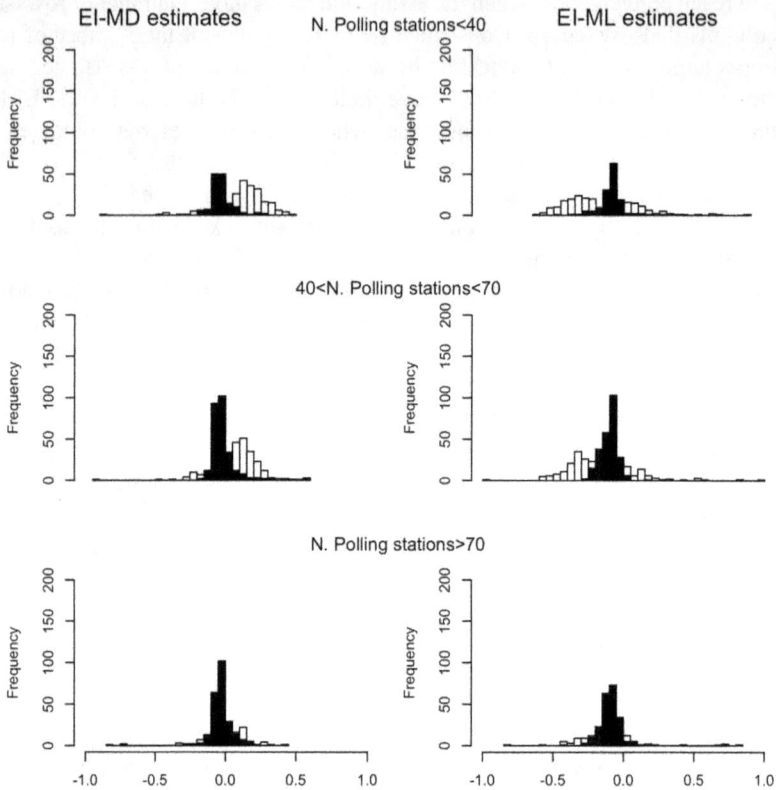

Notes: Difference between district-level estimate and true percentage by number of polling stations; big parties in black and small parties in white color.

I have so far focused on the between-districts variation, that is the difference between estimand and estimate given certain differences across districts. The last feature which is worth investigating is the across unit variance, that is how dissimilar polling stations inside each specific district are. For each district in a specific election-year, I calculate the mean and standard deviation of the vote gained by the winning party and pick the district with the highest and the lowest standard deviation. For the 2008 elections in New Zealand these districts are Northcote with an average of the vote for the winning National party of 0.51 and a standard deviation of 0.06; on the opposite I find the Botany district with an average national vote of 0.55 and a standard deviation of 0.21. Luckily enough the two districts are characterised by a very similar number of polling stations and by the same number of candidates and parties running for elections, which means

Figure 3.4: Difference between estimate and estimand, by number of parties (rows)

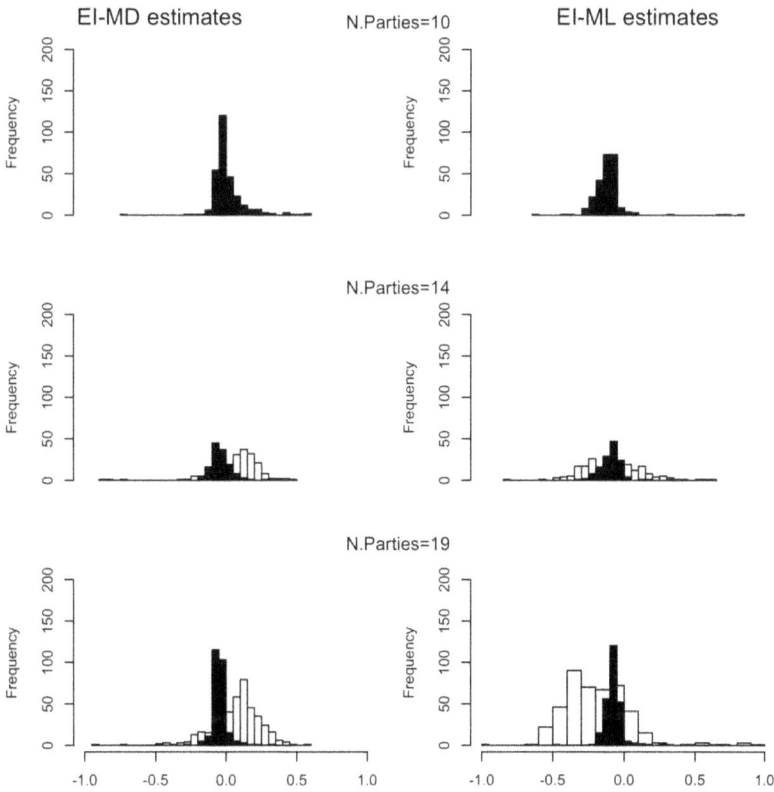

Notes: Difference between district-level estimate and true percentage by number parties; big parties in black and small parties in white colour.

that I can focus just on the extent to which the dissimilarity of the vote affects the quality of the estimates. I then pick two districts from 2002, East Coast Bay and Mana which show similarity and differences to the districts for 2008.[7] The difference between the estimand and the estimates at the party level in each of these two districts is shown in Figure 3.5.

Two main results stand out from Figure 3.5. First, the districts with the highest level of dissimilarity, Botany for the 2008 and Mana for 2002, show higher levels of bias than the districts with the lowest level of dissimilarity, Northcote and East Coast respectively for 2008 and 2002, and this is true for both methods and all parties. When it comes to party-level variation, big parties (here the Labour and

---

7.   It is impossible to present the results for all 280 districts; it should be noticed however, that using other districts or other years of elections report almost identical substantive conclusions.

Figure 3.5: Difference between estimate and estimand, by dissimilarity index

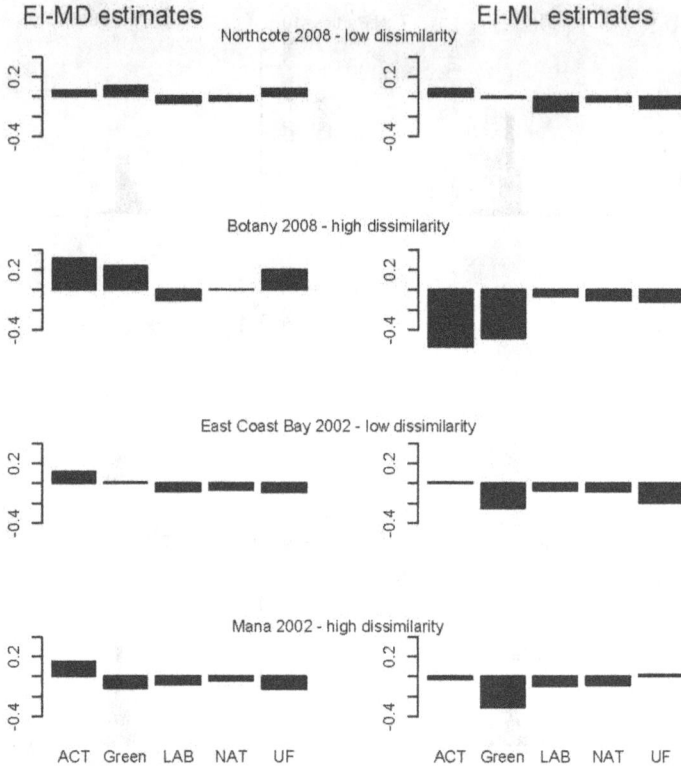

EI-MD estimates   **EI-ML estimates**

Northcote 2008 - low dissimilarity

Botany 2008 - high dissimilarity

East Coast Bay 2002 - low dissimilarity

Mana 2002 - high dissimilarity

ACT Green LAB NAT UF   ACT Green LAB NAT UF

Note: Difference between district-level estimate and true percentage for the district with the highest and lowest variance for the winning party. Key for parties: see main text.

the National parties) show much more precise estimates when compared to the smaller ones (ACT, Green and United Future). Second, across the two methods, the EI-MD appear to outperform the EI-ML in all occasions but also in the case of the EI-MD results, the bias is quite large for small parties in the high dissimilar district of Botany. In particular the estimates for the EI-MD method suffer from an overestimation of straight vote for big parties and an underestimation for small parties. On the other hand, the EI-ML method estimates all suffer from an overestimation of straight vote.

The fact that the error follows a predictable pattern is good news, as it were; indeed, it can be adjusted by, for example, a linear error parameterisation as suggested by Herron and Shotts (2003) or by conditioning the estimates on the standard errors as given by the method as suggested by Adolph *et al.* (2003). This last adjustment is particularly relevant in the context of second-stage regression analysis, which I discuss next.

Second-stage regression models

The estimates provided by the EI-MD and the EI-ML methods, can be used as dependent variables in regression models aim to explain patterns of split-ticket voting at both the district or party level (also referred to as 'second-stage regression' models where in the first stage estimates are obtained and in the second stage these estimates are used as dependent variable in regression models). In my review of the existing literature, the EI-MD or EI-ML estimates have never been used as dependent variables in regression models. However, since they consist of generalisation of 2x2 methods to multi-party settings, I follow the prescriptions of the most recent methodological literature on smaller estimation tables. Concerning the use of King's (1997) estimates, the methodological literature has suggested the use of the estimated proportions as dependent variable in Weighted Least Squares (WLS) regression models.

In detail, both the EI-MD and the EI-ML provide point estimates and associated EI standard errors. A look at the EI standard errors shows that these are consistently larger for smaller parties than for bigger parties. Because the EI standard error tends to be larger for observations with lower information, and because these are also the observations with a larger error compared to the true values, it is then possible to employ WLS to control for this systematic error (Adolph *et al.* 2003). In second-stage WLS models the estimates, i.e. the dependent variable, are weighted by the inverse of the estimates' EI standard error, thus giving greater weight to observations with more precise estimates of straight-ticket voting (see also Burden and Kimball [1998]).

The goal of the methodological discussion is to compare how different substantive findings are when point estimates are used in place of the true values of split-ticket voting where these are not available. Ideally, the values and the significance level of coefficients using the estimated values of ticket-splitting will not be statistically different from the ones using estimates. It needs to be emphasised that this section is not an attempt to provide a complete substantive investigation of split-ticket voting.

The dependent variable for the models presented in Table 3.4 is the proportion of split-ticket voting, true or estimated, for each party at the district level.[8] The models include some of the most common independent variables used by the existing literature on split-ticket voting. Incumbency and gender are both dummy

---

8. For all models presented in Table 3.4 substantive results are unchanged if two-sided Tobit models are estimated to account for a dependent variable censored at 0 and 1 or when using beta regression to account for a dependent variable measured as a proportion. In this regard, Kieschnick and McCullough (2003) after surveying several studies using proportions as dependent variable, find evidence to reject the OLS, the censored normal and the logistic normal models; instead they suggest the adoption of beta regression (see also the discussion in Papke and Wooldridge 1996; Cribari-Neto and Zeileis 2010). I run a similar test of different regression techniques to choose the most appropriate model specification. Details are shown in Appendix 3.III. Here it is sufficient to mention as the choice of the model, i.e. WLS, Tobit or Beta model, does not appear to affect the results, for this reason subsequent investigations of split-ticket voting employ a more straightforward WLS regression.

variables that measure candidate features likely to affect the probability of splitting. I expect incumbency to have a negative effect on split-ticket voting (e.g., Bawn 1999; McAllister and White 2000; Karp *et al.* 2002). Regarding candidate gender instead, Karp (2009) showed that its effect on split-ticket voting is rather low given that female candidates are neither more nor less likely to be characterised by split-ticket voting when compared to their male counterparts. I then add two variables capturing features of the district race likely to impact the amount of split-ticket voting observed in a specific district. I follow existing studies and measure these variables in the previous year of election to avoid the well-know endogeneity problem (see for instance the discussion in Karp *et al.* 2002).

Margin measures the competitiveness of the district race as the difference between the first and second best candidate in each district and the general expectation is a negative effect on ticket-splitting (Cox 1997; Reed 1999). The variable 'DContention' instead measures the percentage difference between that specific party's candidate and the vote for the lowest of the two top SMD contenders, or zero if that candidate ranked first or second (Niemi *et al.* 1992: 232). The expectation is a positive effect if split-ticket voting is to be considered strategic: indeed as the candidate's party is further away from the possibility of winning the district race, the more strategic voters should coordinate deserting this candidate while still supporting that candidate's party on the proportional tier. As already mentioned, in this context I am not interested in the substantive outcome of each of this variable, but rather how different their effect is when modelled using different estimation techniques.

Table 3.4 shows the results of these comparisons. Model 1 reports findings using as dependent variable the true value of split-ticket voting. The results using point estimates derived from the application of the EI-MD and EI- ML methods are shown in Model 2 and 3 respectively. The 'Switch' columns provide pairwise comparisons between the use of the true values and the use of one of the estimation methods. When a 'No' appears in the Switch column, this means that the results are not substantively different when point estimates are used in place of the true values of ticket-splitting. Conversely, when a 'Yes' appears in the Switch column, this means that the results are substantively different.

When it comes to Table 3.4, for the EI-MD models the results are remarkably similar despite differences in the size of the coefficients. Part of the coefficient's significance instead is lost for some variables in the case of the EI-ML model. Results across all years of elections confirm the good performance of the different methods. I ran many more models than those shown here adding and dropping several variables and by pooling data across elections. In all instances, the positive patterns were kept in the overwhelming majority of cases. Overall, it appears that the substitution of the dependent variable with estimated quantities does not change substantive findings especially when using the EI-ML method. Specifically, the EI-MD method provides the best estimation method among those tested in this chapter and it offers an important tool to investigate split-ticket voting at the aggregate-level in subsequent chapters of this book.

Table 3.4: Second-stage regression models: a comparison of estimation methods

Dependent variable:	True values	EI-MD estimates		EI-ML estimates	
	(Model 1)	(Model 2)	Switch	(Model 3)	Switch
	New Zealand	*2002*			
Incumbency	−0.155***	−0.141***	No	−0.015*	No
	(0.023)	(0.033)		(0.006)	
Gender	−0.021	0.023	No	−0.007	No
	(0.022)	(0.032)		(0.008)	
Dcontention	1.219***	2.306***	No	0.735**	No
	(0.124)	(0.160)		(0.241)	
Margin	−0.018	0.116	No	−0.035	No
	(0.080)	(0.129)		(0.022)	
R-squared	0.669	0.825		0.339	
AIC	−327.762	−225.778		−807.026	
	New Zealand	*2005*			
Incumbency	−0.148***	−0.174***	No	−0.010	Yes
	(0.030)	(0.034)		(0.005)	
Gender	−0.004	0.016	No	0.006	No
	(0.020)	(0.038)		(0.004)	
Dcontention	1.936***	3.247***	No	1.351***	No
	(0.137)	(0.185)		(0.218)	
Margin	−0.042	0.166	No	−0.013	No
	(0.074)	(0.131)		(0.016)	
R-squared	0.709	0.818		0.477	
AIC	−310.939	−216.860		−797.707	
	New Zealand	*2008*			
Incumbency	−0.137***	−0.147***	No	−0.004	Yes
	(0.021)	(0.021)		(0.003)	
Gender	−0.014	−0.055***	Yes	0.002	No
	(0.013)	(0.016)		(0.004)	
Dcontention	1.629***	2.292***	No	0.978***	No
	(0.074)	(0.072)		(0.096)	
Margin	0.415***	0.508***	No	−0.007	Yes
	(0.060)	(0.083)		(0.007)	
R−squared	0.803	0.902		0.517	
AIC	−367.808	−384.696		−909.741	

(Continued)

Table 3.4: Second-stage regression models: a comparison of estimation methods (Continued)

Dependent variable:	True values	EI-MD estimates		EI-ML estimates	
	(Model 1)	(Model 2)	Switch	(Model 3)	Switch
	Scotland	*2007*			
Incumbency	−0.063***	−0.015*	No	−0.027*	No
	(0.010)	(0.006)		(0.013)	
Gender	0.002	0.054	No	−0.034	No
	(0.008)	(0.032)		(0.025)	
Dcontention	0.442***	0.570***	No	0.810	Yes
	(0.072)	(0.153)		(0.563)	
Margin	0.027	0.076	No	0.414	No
	(0.048)	(0.066)		(0.378)	
R-squared	0.426	0.123		0.196	
AIC	−705.734	−332.271		−109.456	

Notes: New Zealand (NZ) 2002 observations: 334; NZ 2005 observations: 338; NZ 2008 observations: 313; Scotland 2007 observations: 286.

Summary

Split-ticket voting can be measured both at the individual and at the aggregate-level using respectively surveys and aggregate electoral results. Survey data represents an ideal source to study split-ticket voting if one wants to access voters' preferences and motivations. Notwithstanding, beside the problems of limited sample and over-reporting, current use of surveys to study vote choice under mixed rules has been unsatisfactory. In this chapter I have reviewed in particular the problem associated with limited information on voters' preferences and the reliance on untested (and often unintuitive) assumptions on vote choice when using data at the individual-level. The alternative approaches I take in the book are to study separately the determinants of the two votes and to alter the measurement of the independent variables.

Moving to the aggregate electoral data, I started by highlighting that aggregate electoral results enable one to answer additional questions on split-ticket voting when compared to the exclusive use of surveys. In particular, aggregate data allows us to focus on the party and district-level variation, investigating where and when split-ticket voting is more common. Despite these positive notes however, the use of aggregate data is also plagued by methodological flaws. In this regard, I tested two recent estimation methods able to deal with the well-known ecological fallacy problem. Using exceptional data on the true level of straight and split-ticket voting in New Zealand and Scotland, this chapter provided comprehensive tests of the Rosen *et al.* (2001) and the Greiner and Quinn (2009) methods highlighting their issues and limitations. A few observations are noteworthy.

First, the two techniques perform remarkably well over time and across settings. In particular, since the point estimates are close enough to the true values, when used in regression models, they provide similar results to the ones obtained using the true values. This is an important remark in the light of the fact that the true levels of split-ticket voting are not normally available to the researchers. Because the issue of measurement of split-ticket voting is a common one, the results of this analysis can be regarded as useful in all other settings where researchers have only available aggregate data but they are interested in explaining the variation at a disaggregated level. Since the Rosen *et al.* (2001) method performs best, I will employ this method exclusively for the substantive analyses in the second part of this book. The methodological findings from this chapter provide a fundamental basis for the substantive interpretations of split-ticket voting conducted in the rest of the book.

PART II

EMPIRICAL EVIDENCE: WHY AND
HOW VOTERS SPLIT THEIR VOTE

Chapter Four

A Cross-Country Analysis of Split-Ticket Voting

This chapter aims to address two limitations within the existing literature of vote choice under mixed systems. First, in the outset of this book it was mentioned that as of today there is a lack of comparative studies. Cross-national comparison is essential since the generalisations based on one specific country experience may be inapplicable to other cases. This may be due to the specifics of the electoral rules, where the linkage between the two tiers of the ballot paper may alter the incentives to engage in a specific form of strategic behaviour. In addition, country-level factors such as prior experience with the electoral rules and levels of party institutionalisation may alter voters' propensity and capacity to act on certain incentives provided by the electoral rules. Second, another important limitation with existing studies is their reliance on the assumption that the voter's party vote comes first; the voter is defined as a supporter of that party, whose vote choice on the majoritarian ballot can then be analysed to see if the voter follows that party or not. In fact, the party vote is an endogenous product of an election in which the voter is also being asked to vote for a candidate, and one must recognise that some voters may start by choosing a majoritarian candidate and follow the candidate to a party with their PR vote. In extremely party-oriented election systems like Italy's or Germany's, it may be reasonable to assume that most voters start with at least a loose attachment to a party, but in mixed systems that are newer to PR voting, where new parties form and disappear frequently, and where many voters are non-aligned, such voters may not be in a minority.

The lack of comparative investigations and the reliance on untested assumptions in the current literature call for both a cross-country and a cross-vote analysis. From a comparative point of view, this chapter analyses vote choice in nine mixed-member electoral systems covering all possible combinations of mixed rules, i.e., mixed-proportional and mixed-majoritarian, at the national and sub-national level spanning several years of election for each country. The focus is on five established democracies, the national elections in Germany, New Zealand, Japan, Italy and the sub-national elections in Scotland. The analysis employs mixed-level datasets where individual-level data about voters' preferences and motivations are combined with district-level information, which takes into account the electoral context in which the vote is cast. Additional comparisons will be provided for Albania, Hungary, Thailand and South Korea. (See Appendix 4.I for data sources).[1]

Furthermore, the analysis conducted in this chapter relaxes the assumption concerning the primacy of the party vote on both tiers of the ballot paper by investigating the two votes separately rather than in conjunction, as is the practice in the existing literature. This means that the analysis will not consider directly whether the voter casts a split or a straight vote. It rather assesses how different the two votes are when it comes to several voting behaviour determinants using both pre- and post-electoral data. As far as I can tell, neither a comparative investigation of individual preferences across all types of mixed systems nor a comparative investigation of the two votes have been conducted before.

The chapter is structured as follows. I start presenting theoretical expectations regarding voting behaviour and explaining the empirical strategies. Then I discuss the independent variables and their measurement. Following this I discuss the results of the two empirical approaches, while in the discussion section I connect the two levels of analysis.

Explaining vote choice

Sincere voting describes a situation in which an individual casts a vote for the preferred party or candidate irrespective of expectations about the election outcome (Fisher 2004). The question of what makes certain parties more attractive than others has been addressed long ago. Preferences for parties can be based on affective social identifications (Campbell and Miller 1957) or, in a Downsian world of rational political behaviour (Downs 1957), they might be based on ideology and policy preferences. What about candidates? Theoretically, it could be postulated that candidates' preference follows, first of all, from party preference but deviations from this could be expected where candidate appeals may be in conflict with that for parties. There are many ways in which candidate appeal can become salient; perhaps the most widely recognised is incumbency (Banducci et al. 1998; Burden and Kimball 2004). The more incentives and opportunities there are for candidates to personalise their links with voters, the more likely it is that preferences for party and candidate may conflict in the mind of the voter.

Conversely, strategic voters are those who do not vote in line with their preferences since they are primarily concerned with expectations about how parties or candidates will perform at the elections. Cox (1997: 194) develops and organises these ideas by outlining two different strategic incentives: the classical

---

1. The sample of countries covered in this chapter includes all mixed systems for which electoral surveys are readily available. For the sake of completeness, other countries adopting mixed rules not included in this work because of lack of reliable individual-level data are, in Europe: Lithuania, Ukraine and Russia; in Asia: Taiwan, Armenia, Azerbaijan, Georgia, Kazakistan, Pakistan, Philippines, Taijikistan, and Timor-Este; Bolivia and Venezuela in Latin America and Lesotho, Guinea, Senegal, Seychelles in Africa.

'wasted vote' and 'threshold insurance' strategic voting.[2] The wasted vote, i.e. the vote for a larger party when the one preferred by the voter is at risk of not being represented in parliament, has been extensively examined (e.g., Blais *et al.* 2001; 2005; Alvarez and Nagler 2000; Franklin *et al.* 1994). Threshold insurance strategic voting has recently been gaining attention: this second type of strategic voting occurs when supporters of large parties vote for a small party that is part of an expected coalition in order to make the coalition as a whole succeed (Gschwend 2007). While the wasted vote is more common under plurality systems, threshold-insurance strategic voting can arguably be seen in proportional systems where there is an electoral threshold and a history of coalition governments (Abramson *et al.* 2010; Fredén 2014).

Given that voters cast two votes, one under plurality and one under proportional rules, the two types of strategic voting, i.e. the wasted vote and the threshold insurance vote, are equally and concurrently possible under mixed-member systems. Be that as it may, both votes or just one of them are simply sincerely cast. Hence, as extensively explained in Chapter Three, the categories of straight- and split-ticket voting are insufficient to distinguish between sincere and strategic voting. What one can say, in fact, is that these two forms of strategic voting are sufficient conditions of split-ticket voting, but there are other causes, primarily a misalignment of preferences for parties and candidates. At the same time, sincere and straight vote do not need to be identical given that a supporter of a small party, who perceived this party to have no chance on either of the ballot papers, may indeed decide to cast a straight vote instead (Pappi and Thurner 2002).

This chapter deals with the limitations of using the category of split and straight vote to analyse vote choice under mixed rules, employing two different empirical strategies where both are based on the idea of investigating the two votes separately rather than in conjunction, as explained next.

Data and methods

First, this chapter investigates whether, and to what extent, the two votes are different with regard to observed patterns between the pre- and post-electoral setting by comparing intended and actual vote choice.[3] Usually, the change of preferences before and after an election concerns the electorate's response to the more or less immediate circumstances that surround a specific election (e.g., Wlezien and Erikson 2001; Hillygus and Jackman 2003). In this chapter, the primary interest is not on the reasons why voters change their mind before and after the elections. Rather the focus is on assessing how different intentions and

---

2.   In fact, Cox (1997) outlines several more strategic incentives. Here, however, I only consider the two incentives that are most commonly examined in the literature on mixed-member electoral systems.

3.   In line with common practice, I exclude from the analysis voters who cast a vote solely for a party or solely for a candidate; these voters represent less than 5% of the sample included in the election studies at hand.

actual vote choice are and whether or not there are any meaningful differences between the patterns observed in the party and the candidate vote. Since both votes are cast by the same voter and during the same election, the general expectation is that I should not see major differences across the two votes. On the other hand, if one of the two votes is more likely to change during the electoral campaign than the other, I will wonder why by examining specific factors related to sincere and strategic voting.

The second step consists in looking only at actual vote choice providing a comparative investigation of the two votes. The aim is to assess what explains the two votes and if there are substantial differences when it comes to the influence of sincere, strategic and institutional factors. All the independent variables are measured at time *t-1* while the dependent variable, i.e., vote choice, is measured at the post-electoral stage. Pre-electoral data are needed since they allow us to measure the independent variables of interest before the elections take place. The use of pre-electoral data stems from the problem that responses given after the elections are more likely to be affected by the election results (see also the discussion in Carman and Johns [2010] and Fredén [2014]). The analysis draws upon nine countries as listed in Table 4.1: the national elections in Albania, Germany, Hungary, Italy, Japan, New Zealand, Thailand, South Korea, and two sub-state elections in Scotland.

Table 4.1: Countries, rules and variation

Country	Tiers combination	Period of application	Years covered in this chapter	Ticket-splitting (Min-Max %)
Albania	Mixed-Proportional	1997–2007	2005	40–50
Germany	Mixed-Proportional	1949-present	2009–2013	25–35
Hungary	Mixed-Semi-Majoritarian	1990-present	1998–2002	15–20
Italy	Mixed-Semi-Majoritarian	1994–2001	1996–2001	20–45
Japan	Mixed-Majoritarian	1996-present	1996–2005	25–40
New Zealand	Mixed-Proportional	1996-present	1996–2002	25–50
Scotland	Mixed-Proportional	1999-present	2007–2011	20–30
South Korea	Mixed-Majoritarian	1988-present*	2004–2008	10–30
Thailand	Mixed-Majoritarian	2001-present	2007	10–20

Notes: Minimum and maximum levels of split-ticket voting calculated by country across all years of election covered in this chapter.

* Only in 2004, after the Constitutional Court ruled against the one-vote system South Korea implemented the more common two-vote variety of mixed system. Before that the country adopted a one-vote mixed system with a strong majoritarian thrust.

The sample of countries allows significant variation on several features that might have an impact on vote choice. First, the group of countries covers all possible combinations of mixed rules: mixed-majoritarian and semi-majoritarian, mixed- proportional and semi-proportional;[4] furthermore, it includes both national and sub-state elections. The sample of countries analysed allows variation on familiarity with the electoral rules: in particular, Germany used its mixed systems since 1949 while in other countries, such as Thailand, the system has been introduced only more recently. The countries are also different with regard to patterns of split-ticket voting. Table 4.1 shows that split-ticket voting appears to be higher in New Zealand, Albania and other mixed-proportional systems when compared to mixed-majoritarian systems such as South Korea and Thailand. Also, in countries like Hungary and Scotland there is much less variation in the overall amount of split-ticket voting across elections when compared to some other countries such as Italy, Japan and New Zealand. I will explain below how the variation on these dimensions is expected to influence vote choice in the two tiers of the ballot paper.

Expectations

Starting with the issue of voter sincerity, it makes sense to analyse the extent to which (sincere) preferences for parties and candidates explain the two votes. On a general level, I would expect that parties' preferences matter more on the PR when compared to candidate preferences which are expected to be more important on the SMD vote. When it comes to preferences for parties, I use a measure of party attachment built using the traditional question: 'Do you usually think of yourself as close to any political party?' ('PID' variable). It is also possible to use frequently available feeling thermometer questions asking respondents to provide a score for the parties on a scale from '0' to '10' where '10' means 'like the party very much' ('Party Sympathy').

Moving to candidates, isolating the effect of sincere candidates' preferences on vote choice is rather difficult. On the one hand, surveys provide researchers with questions on preferences for parties but comparable questions are not usually available for candidates (see also the discussion in Herrmann and Pappi 2008). On the other hand, the use of aggregate indicators to measure preferences for candidates, including incumbency, is problematic as it does not help disentangling individual-level strategic motivations from more sincere ones. Thus, elevated support for incumbent candidates, for instance, may be due to their personal qualities as well as to the fact that they are relatively more likely to get elected than challenger candidates. To assess the impact of candidates, this chapter gives attention to their key features, such as incumbency ('Incumbency' variable). In addition, I check the

---

4. The configuration of the Italian (D'Alimonte 2005) and Hungarian (Benoit 2005) systems makes it harder to classify them. Both systems are a special version of mixed-majoritarian rules, also defined as semi-majoritarian mixed systems (Cox and Schoppa 2002). For details on the classification of existing mixed systems see Shugart and Wattenberg (2003).

effect of district-level indicators, as discussed next, to disentangle personal voting for candidates from strategic district-level motivations.

Niemi *et al.* (1992: 232), among others, suggest the use of aggregate variables to measure strategic voting, primarily district competitiveness, when individual-level expectations about the election outcome are not available.[5] The competitiveness of the district race is measured as the difference between the first and second best performing candidate in each district. When the district race is more competitive, strategic supporters of the two top-ranked candidates should stick with their candidates to guarantee their victory. On the other hand, an opposite result may indicate the presence of personal voting, especially for the second-placed candidate, because strategically, there is no reason to support a candidate that has no chance of winning. Of course this non-strategic straight vote can come about for other reasons, such as protest voting; despite this, however, the effect of candidate-specific factors is arguably the most important (Moser and Scheiner 2005: 263) ('Margin' variable).

Earlier I pointed out that strategic voting is potentially to be seen both in the majoritarian and proportional part of the ballot paper. In the first instance, I created a variable that measured for each party's candidate the percentage difference between that candidate and the vote for the lowest of the two top contenders, or zero if that candidate ranked first or second ('DContention_SMD' variable). As mentioned in previous chapters, the expectation is a positive effect: the lower the difference between the vote for one's most preferred candidate and the lower of the two top contenders, the less likely an individual should be to switch from her party and vote strategically for one of the two top contenders. When it comes to strategic voting on the PR tier, I include two variables. First and foremost, I include a variable simply measuring the percentage of the party vote received by that party in the previous year of elections ('DContention_PR' variable). Second, I add a direct measure of coalition preferences: to this end I create a variable that scores 1 when the party is either included in a respondent's most preferred coalition and/or a respondent wishes that party to form a government after the elections ('Coalition Sympathy' variable).[6] Notwithstanding, voters' decision to react strategically depends on their capacity to cope and understand the context in which the vote is cast (Gschwend 2007). For this reason it makes sense to control for several factors correlated with a strategic reaction to the electoral rules, primarily education. Finally I control for age and gender.

When it comes to institutional variation, there are two main variants of mixed systems: they can be mixed-proportional or mixed-majoritarian. A few other mixed

5.   Unfortunately for the countries analysed in this chapter, only in 2002 in New Zealand, 2007 in Scotland, and several elections in Japan did pre-electoral surveys ask questions on voter expectations for each party and candidate running for elections. In these countries response patterns indicate that not all of those intended to vote for a candidate are purely strategic. However, those who vote for a candidate generally think (correctly or not) that this candidate has a good chance of winning the district seat.

6.   Ideally I would have wanted to also control for respondents' evaluation of the chances for a coalition to take place after the election (see also the discussion in Blais *et al.* 2006). However, in only about half of the countries under scrutiny in this chapter is such a question available.

systems are hard to classify in one of these two groups and for this reason they are often defined as semi-proportional or semi-majoritarian mixed systems (Shugart and Wattenberg 2003). Naturally, the features of the electoral systems affect the amount of strategic party and candidate votes. In mixed-proportional systems, a candidate vote is less important to the outcome of the elections. It has therefore been argued that the perceived costs of a strategic candidate vote are lower in mixed-proportional than in mixed-majoritarian systems (Gschwend 2007: 10). Everything else being equal, one should thus observe more strategic candidate votes in Albania, Germany, New Zealand and Scotland than in the other countries. Secondly, parties in mixed-majoritarian systems have a much stronger incentive to focus on winning as many SMDs as possible because these are more important for the electoral outcome. Consequently, personal voting is expected to be higher in these systems when compared to mixed-proportional systems (Moser and Scheiner 2005).

Among the countries analysed, Germany has used a mixed system for decades, but the system is quite new in other countries. Voters' experience with the electoral rules is likely to influence their strategic coordination (Cox and Schoppa 2002) thus holding everything else constant, strategic voting should be the highest in Germany. Furthermore existing works often suggest that the lack of party system institutionalisation is probably the reason strategic voting is very low in less developed democracies (Kostadinova 2002; Moser and Scheiner 2009). Germany, New Zealand, Japan and Italy are consolidated democracies but democracy and a stable party system are relatively new, at least for the elections analysed in this chapter: Hungary, Albania and South Korea. Thailand instead is still not considered to be a fully developed democracy (e.g., Norris 2005). Thus, everything else being equal, I expect higher strategic coordination in Germany, New Zealand, Japan, Italy and Scotland when compared to Hungary, Albania, South Korea and Thailand, where I expect the influence of sincere voting determinants to matter more than in the first group of countries.

In relation to the only sub-national setting included in the analysis, one expects strategic voting to be comparatively lower in Scotland than in the other countries. This expectation is based on the idea that a non-general election might be regarded by voters (at least to some extent) as less important than a national election and this would lead to either less concern for voters about wasting their vote or the perception that these elections might offer a chance to experiment by supporting smaller parties. Despite Curtice finding no support for the 'experiment hypothesis' in the Scottish context (Curtice 2006: 119), the fact that in Scotland smaller parties tend on average to perform better in sub-state elections than in national elections, would suggest the presence of lower strategic incentives in the sub-state setting.

Empirical analysis

The empirical analysis examines the two votes, the party and the candidate vote, separately, rather than in conjunction, as is the practice in the existing literature. In this regard, I follow two strategies.

Comparing the pre- and post-electoral vote

The analysis in this section compares intentions and actual vote in the PR and SMD vote. Table 4.2 lists the countries starting from most proportional to most majoritarian mixed systems. First, the analysis compares Intentional (I) and Actual (A) vote on the PR using correlation coefficients. Then the same difference (I versus A) is considered examining the candidate vote. Subsequently, because the aim is to assess if there are meaningful differences across the two votes, I compare the two correlation coefficients to assess whether or not there are significant differences between the two correlation coefficients.[7] When the difference showed in Table 4.2 is positive, it means that the intended and actual PR vote is more similar than the intended and actual SMD vote. In other words, the PR vote is more stable across the pre- and post-election setting than the SMD vote. Bold coefficients are a sign that this difference is statistically significant. Table 4.2 indicates that the PR vote is to some extent more stable than the SMD vote (positive difference) everywhere except in Japan where the opposite holds true (negative difference). However, the differences are pretty small and only significant in Japan (negative difference) and New Zealand (positive difference), except in 1996.

Second, I calculate a correlation coefficient between intended PR and intended SMD and then compare this to the correlation coefficient obtained comparing the actual PR and the actual SMD vote. The aim of this step is to check more generally how different voting intention and actual vote choice are and whether PR and SMD vote are more similar before or after the elections. When the coefficient displayed in the table is positive and significant it means that the PR and the SMD votes are more similar in the pre-electoral setting than after the elections. In other words, I find less split-ticket voting prior to the elections. The second part of Table 4.2 suggests that again the difference between the two votes is very low; in the rare cases the difference is significant it is positive in mixed-proportional systems and negative in mixed-majoritarian systems. This means that in the majority of cases, split-ticket voting is, at least to some extent, a consequence of the electoral campaign – except in Italy.

It is possible to examine these patterns further, checking whether or not these results hold for specific subgroups of voters. For instance, one may compare voters holding long-term party identification with non-identifiers under the expectation that voters in the former group are more likely to show stable patterns overall. Full results are presented in Appendix 4.II, while here I only report substantive conclusions. The findings indicate that identifiers are slightly less likely to change their mind during the election campaign and more likely to cast a straight vote than non-identifiers. This effect is indicated by higher correlation coefficients for party identifiers when compared to non-identifiers and by lower differences overall for the first group of voters. In all mixed-proportional systems the differences between the PR and SMD across the subgroups of identifiers and non-identifiers are not

---

7.   The *Fisher r-to-z transformation* is used to obtain a value of *z* that can be applied to assess the significance of the difference between two correlation coefficients (Zar 1996).

statistically significant. In Italy and Japan instead these differences are negative and often statistically significant. This suggests that in both countries the candidate vote is at least as stable between the pre- and post-electoral setting as the party vote. The stability of the candidate vote can be a consequence of personal voting, as voters value candidate higher than parties; or it can be due to the fact that voters know prior to the elections how to cast their candidate vote, being clearly instructed by parties to follow their pre-electoral agreements. Both explanations can be valid and I will come back to this in following sections of this chapter.

One could also look at those respondents whose party, they intended to vote for or have voted for, ranked first or second in the previous election. As mentioned earlier, the expectation is that the lower the difference between the vote for one's most preferred candidate and the lower of the two top contenders, less likely an individual should be to switch from their party and vote strategically for one of the two top contenders to avoid wasting the vote (Niemi *et al.* 1992). Given that it is very likely that wasting vote considerations are formed during the electoral campaign (e.g., Johnston and Pattie 2002), if those voting for a bigger party truly prefer this party, I should find them to be less likely to change their mind or cast a split vote. If, on the other hand, this group of respondents shows less stable patterns between the intended and actual vote, this can be considered a sign of strategic vote. The results vary across countries but overall the patterns of the two subgroups of voters are extremely similar and the differences between the two votes rarely statistically significant. There are, however, interesting differences across mixed-proportional and mixed-majoritarian systems. First, it is worth noticing that correlation coefficients are generally higher in Japan and Italy when compared to Germany, Scotland and New Zealand, a sign again that the two votes are more similar in Italy and Japan. Second, in Japan and Italy only, there are significant differences across the two votes for both subgroups of voters where those supporting lower-ranked parties only are more likely to split or change their mind but more often on the PR rather than in the SMD vote, which is again most probably a sign of personal voting.

To sum up, across countries, identifiers are unsurprisingly less likely to change their mind during the electoral campaign and more likely to cast a straight vote. Regarding those respondents supporting bigger parties, the analysis indicates a difference between mixed-proportional and mixed-majoritarian systems. In mixed-proportional systems such as Germany there is a clearer indication of strategic voting since those who voted for a big party are less likely to vote for the party or candidate they said that they intended to vote for. In mixed-majoritarian systems, such as Japan and Italy, voters are slightly more likely to change their mind in the party vote rather than in the candidate vote. This finding can be an indication of the presence of either personal voting or 'selective entry' by parties (see also Burden 2009). Indeed, personal voting is expected to be stronger in mixed-majoritarian systems where parties have strong incentives to ask candidates to behave in a more personalistic manner. The finding that in Japan only the SMD vote is even more stable than the PR vote suggests that this is indeed the case. Concerning selective entry, parties

Table 4.2: Correlation between intended and actual vote choice

	Germany		New Zealand			Scotland		Italy	Japan	
	2009	2013	1996	1999	2002	2007	2011	2001	2003	2005
Intended and Actual PR	0.765	0.891	0.593	0.613	0.598	0.831	0.899	0.794	0.818	0.807
Intended and Actual SMD	0.761	0.878	0.596	0.563	0.527	0.827	0.887	0.775	0.873	0.906
diff	*0.004*	*0.013*	*−0.003*	***0.050***	***0.071***	*0.004*	*0.011*	*0.018*	***−0.055***	***−0.099***
Intended PR and Intended SMD	0.720	0.848	0.430	0.320	0.415	0.755	0.836	0.820	0.656	0.637
Actual PR and Actual SMD	0.669	0.855	0.399	0.248	0.365	0.772	0.844	0.879	0.625	0.659
diff	***0.051***	*−0.007*	*0.031*	***0.072***	*0.049*	*−0.017*	*−0.007*	***−0.059***	*0.031*	*−0.022*
N	2042	3213	1377	1522	1147	834	512	1901	795	843

Notes: Data sources are listed in the Appendix 4.I.

usually contest more SMDs in Germany and New Zealand than they do in the Italian and Japanese settings where they often engage in formal pre-electoral coalition agreements. The fact that the SMD vote is more stable across elections in Japan may indicate that party competition at the district level is increasingly institutionalised in this country.

Comparing the two votes

The second step consists in analysing the two votes using multivariate analysis. The dependent variable is actual vote choice, as measured in the post-electoral stage, while all the independent variables are measured using pre-electoral data. Attention is given to what explains vote choice in two parts of the electoral ballot and whether or not there are meaningful differences between the two votes. Each model comprises several basic determinants of vote choice: party attachment, sympathy for parties and coalitions, incumbency, national chances for parties and local chances for candidates and district competitiveness.

As one can assume that specific voters' evaluations have an effect on all potential parties and not only on particular ones, modelling all potential choices in one model offers a general picture of the effect of these evaluations. Thus, the data set is expanded by the number of parties available in our surveys. In this 'stacked' dataset, vote choice serves as a dependent variable, with each respondent contributing a certain number of observations, one for each of the parties available in the survey. Vote choice is a categorical variable with multiple outcomes, which is why a maximum likelihood model is suitable (Long 1997). In multinomial logit, individual specific characteristics, such as education, can be included in the model and regressed on different outcomes. An extension of this method is conditional logit, in which choice-specific variables, for which the respondent's scores vary for the different alternatives, can also be included in the analysis as well. In the extended conditional logit model, individual-specific variables can also be included. The conditional logit model can be expressed as a vote utility function, which aims to capture the benefits the voter receives from voting for a party (see Alvarez and Nagler 1998):

$$U_{ij} = \beta X_{ij} + \psi_j a_i + u_{ij}$$

where U_{ij} is the utility for individual i to vote for alternative, j; X_{ij} are the choice-specific variables with different values for individual i and alternative j and coefficient β; a_i are the individual-specific variables with different values for individual i and different coefficients ψ for all alternatives j. u_{ij} is an error term of factors unexplained by the model.

The coefficients for the choice-specific variables are the same for all alternatives and measure the mean impact of a variable on party choice. For example, the party preference variable measures how much a voter likes party X using a scale from '0' (do not like the party) to '10' (like the party very much). Each respondent gets a different value for each party, and the probability to vote for a specific alternative is expected to be affected by this preference. In contrast, the individual-specific variables have different coefficients for all possible outcomes in the model. This implies that an increase in, for example, the level of education may be positively related to voting for one party, but negatively related to voting for another party. It should be noticed that for all countries, except Italy, I use pooled data covering more than one year of elections. I do not show results relative to a specific year of elections because running models separately returns the same substantive conclusions: while results are of course slightly different for each election-year, substantive conclusions about the probability of casting a specific vote holds across elections.

For each country, Table 4.3 shows the relationship between vote choice in the two parts of the electoral ballot, and vote-choice determinants. Firstly, across all countries, being an identifier increases the chances of voting for a specific party and for a specific candidate; this probability is generally higher for the party rather than for the candidate vote and especially so in Japan and Italy. There are, however, some conspicuous differences across countries: party identification has a higher effect in Germany when compared to the other countries and a high effect also in Italy, but only in the PR vote. Party sympathy also has a statistically positive effect

Table 4.3: Vote choice and its determinants: conditional logit models, sample 1

	Germany (2009–2013)		New Zealand (1996–2002)		Scotland (2007–2011)		Japan (2003–2005)		Italy (2001)	
	VOTE PR	VOTE SMD	VOTE PR	VOTE SMD	VOTE PR	VOTE SMD	VOTE PR	VOTE SMD	VOTE PR	VOTE SMD
Choice-specific										
PID	1.48***	1.37***	0.83***	0.66***	0.84***	0.78***	0.82***	0.59***	1.91***	0.89***
	(0.04)	(0.04)	(0.07)	(0.06)	(0.14)	(0.12)	(0.11)	(0.12)	(0.19)	(0.15)
Party Sympathy	0.52***	0.44***	0.90***	0.54***	0.56***	0.45***	0.40***	0.29***	4.79***	3.40***
	(0.02)	(0.01)	(0.02)	(0.01)	(0.04)	(0.03)	(0.03)	(0.03)	(0.32)	(0.21)
Incumbency	0.03	0.20***	−0.01	0.05	0.17	0.42***	0.08	0.33*	0.01	0.44**
	(0.05)	(0.05)	(0.07)	(0.06)	(0.12)	(0.11)	(0.17)	(0.14)	(0.13)	(0.15)
Coalition Sympathy	1.14***	1.00***	0.14*	0.27***	1.08***	0.90***	0.77***	1.12***		
	(0.06)	(0.06)	(0.06)	(0.05)	(0.20)	(0.17)	(0.12)	(0.13)		
DContention	5.25***	−0.98**	1.81*	−5.24***	2.47*	−2.24***	−4.08	−4.07***	−4.95	−6.88***
	(0.43)	(0.36)	(0.79)	(0.40)	(1.06)	(0.64)	(2.32)	(0.74)	(3.85)	(1.81)
Individual-specific	Ref: CDU		Ref: Labour		Ref: Conservative		Ref: LDP		Ref: AN	
	SPD		National		Labour		DPJ		CCD-CDU	
Margin	−0.16	−0.79	−0.96	0.87	2.84	0.54	0.24	−0.32	0.12	−4.51
	(0.50)	(0.45)	(0.60)	(0.48)	(1.51)	(1.36)	(0.68)	(0.66)	(4.04)	(3.16)
Age	0.00	0.01*	−0.00	−0.00	−0.01	−0.01	0.00	−0.00	0.03	−0.01
	(0.00)	(0.00)	(0.00)	(0.00)	(0.01)	(0.01)	(0.01)	(0.01)	(0.02)	(0.01)
Education	0.20	0.57***	−0.06	−0.20	−0.38	0.33	0.19	0.38	1.51	1.15
	(0.15)	(0.13)	(0.24)	(0.19)	(0.48)	(0.43)	(0.31)	(0.28)	(0.81)	(0.65)

(Continued)

Table 4.3: *Vote choice and its determinants: conditional logit models, sample 1 (Continued)*

	Germany (2009–2013)		New Zealand (1996–2002)		Scotland (2007–2011)		Japan (2003–2005)		Italy (2001)	
	VOTE PR	VOTE SMD	VOTE PR	VOTE SMD	VOTE PR	VOTE SMD	VOTE PR	VOTE SMD	VOTE PR	VOTE SMD
Female	-0.41***	-0.32***	0.00	-0.07	0.39	0.39	0.15	0.07	-0.20	0.08
	(0.10)	(0.09)	(0.14)	(0.11)	(0.30)	(0.27)	(0.18)	(0.17)	(0.59)	(0.44)
	FDP		Green		Lib Dem		CGP		DS	
Margin	-0.23	-0.78	-0.76	-2.00**	2.61	-1.11	-0.33	-10.74***	1.17	0.24
	(0.55)	(0.68)	(0.69)	(0.67)	(1.59)	(1.48)	(0.98)	(3.10)	(2.94)	(2.33)
Age	-0.00	-0.01	0.00	0.01	0.00	0.01	0.00	0.01	0.01	-0.01
	(0.00)	(0.00)	(0.00)	(0.00)	(0.01)	(0.01)	(0.01)	(0.01)	(0.01)	(0.01)
Education	0.35*	0.16	0.10	-0.27	-0.40	0.86	-0.34	-0.93	-0.28	-0.17
	(0.16)	(0.20)	(0.29)	(0.27)	(0.50)	(0.46)	(0.46)	(0.74)	(0.56)	(0.44)
Female	-0.18	0.11	-0.37*	0.03	0.32	0.28	0.26	0.05	-0.29	-0.06
	(0.12)	(0.14)	(0.16)	(0.15)	(0.31)	(0.28)	(0.26)	(0.43)	(0.40)	(0.32)
	Green		NZF		SNP		SDP		FI	
Margin	-0.89	-0.47	-0.26	-4.57***	3.21*	1.83	-2.18	1.94	0.62	-2.23
	(0.57)	(0.58)	(0.80)	(0.88)	(1.44)	(1.29)	(1.60)	(1.90)	(2.03)	(1.68)
Age	-0.01**	-0.01**	-0.00	-0.01	0.00	0.00	0.00	-0.01	-0.01	-0.01
	(0.00)	(0.00)	(0.01)	(0.01)	(0.01)	(0.01)	(0.01)	(0.03)	(0.01)	(0.01)
Education	0.46**	0.20	0.00	0.59	-0.41	0.36	1.72**	1.11	-0.59	-0.36
	(0.18)	(0.18)	(0.29)	(0.30)	(0.45)	(0.40)	(0.66)	(1.30)	(0.40)	(0.34)
Female	-0.22	-0.08	-0.18	-0.01	0.45	0.16	0.70	1.73*	0.09	0.16
	(0.12)	(0.12)	(0.18)	(0.18)	(0.27)	(0.25)	(0.39)	(0.85)	(0.28)	(0.24)

(Continued)

Table 4.3: Vote choice and its determinants: conditional logit models, sample 1 (Continued)

	Germany (2009–2013)		New Zealand (1996–2002)		Scotland (2007–2011)		Japan (2003–2005)		Italy (2001)	
	VOTE PR	VOTE SMD	VOTE PR	VOTE SMD	VOTE PR	VOTE SMD	VOTE PR	VOTE SMD	VOTE PR	VOTE SMD
	Die Linke		ACT				JCP		LN	
Margin	-0.57	-1.83*	-0.59	-1.64*			-1.47	-2.82	2.45	7.20
	(0.70)	(0.72)	(0.70)	(0.68)			(1.56)	(1.49)	(4.93)	(3.73)
Age	0.00	0.01*	0.00	-0.01			0.02	0.00	-0.02	-0.00
	(0.00)	(0.00)	(0.01)	(0.00)			(0.01)	(0.01)	(0.02)	(0.01)
Education	0.33	0.37	0.13	-0.00			0.81	0.08	-0.45	0.59
	(0.20)	(0.20)	(0.30)	(0.29)			(0.58)	(0.55)	(0.86)	(0.66)
Female	-0.42**	-0.18	-0.54***	0.17			0.04	-0.24	0.73	0.43
	(0.14)	(0.14)	(0.16)	(0.15)			(0.36)	(0.35)	(0.61)	(0.47)
N	32385	32385	20235	20235	5400	5400	5210	5210	5385	5385
LL	-4235.09	-4230.67	-2156.33	-2729.64	-594.81	-729.28	-887.04	-743.66	-392.53	-629.53
AIC	8520.17	8511.34	4362.66	5509.28	1229.61	1498.56	1824.09	1537.32	831.06	1307.07

Notes: Dependent variables are vote choice in the PR and SMD respectively. Source: see Appendix to this chapter. Key to parties: Germany: Christian Democratic Union (CDU), Social Democratic Party (SPD), Free Democratic Party (FDP), Greens, Die Linke; New Zealand: Labour, National, Green, New First (NZF), Association of Consumers and Taxpayers (ACT); Scotland: Conservative, labour, Liberal Democrats (Lib Dem), Scottish National Party (SNP); Japan: Liberal Democratic Party (LDP), Democratic Party of Japan (DPJ), Komeino–Clean Government Party (CGP), Social Democratic Party (SDP), Japanese Communist Party (JCP); Italy: National Alliance (AN), CCD-CDU; Democrats of the Left (DS), Go Italy (FI), Norther League (LN). Estimations performed using the asclogit-command in Stata version 13. Standard errors in parentheses: *p<.05, **p<.01, ***p<.001.

on the probability of voting for a specific party or candidate and also in this case the effect is larger in the PR vote when compared to the SMD vote.[8]

There are then some variables that the literature stresses as pertaining primarily to the party or candidate level. Starting with the incumbency variable, having won that district before should have a much stronger effect on the SMD when compared to the PR vote: this is indeed what I find, except for with New Zealand: in all countries incumbency has a positive effect on vote choice but a stronger effect on the SMD vote. Regarding the variable DContention, it is measured differently in the two votes. In the candidate vote, DContention measures the difference between one's preferred party and the second best placed candidate in the district using data from the previous year of election. If voters are strategic the coefficient of this variable should be negative, and this is what I find. With regard to the PR vote, DContention measures the percentage of votes received by the party at the national level in the previous year of election. For this reason, the variable should measure the probability of casting a PR vote for a party according to the party national size. If the effect is positive it simply indicates that bigger parties are more likely to receive a vote on the PR ballot. On the other hand, a negative coefficient indicates that the larger the party, the smaller the probability of voting for that party on the PR tier. This will suggest a certain degree of strategic reasoning in line with the coalition voting hypothesis. DContention in the party vote is found to be positive and significant everywhere; its effect is very high and similar to DContention in the SMD vote, except in Italy and Japan where the variable is not statistically significant. The variable measuring coalition preferences is also statistically significant everywhere being at least as strong in the SMD as in the PR, except for Germany where it is stronger on the PR vote.

Moving to the individual-specific variables, Margin measures the difference between the first and second-placed candidate in a district. This variable is used as a control for the competitiveness of the district race and it is expected a) to have a stronger effect in the SMD vote when compared to the PR vote and b) to be positive for big parties if one ought to conclude that strategic voting is present at the district level. The variable is usually not statistically significant and if so, it is significant for small parties and of negative sign. This result means that support for strategic considerations is very low across all countries.

To sum up, first, the analysis made it clear that party-level determinants tend to be more important in explaining the party when compared to the candidate vote. Second, the local context seems to play a larger role on the candidate vote. Similarly, the candidate vote appears only slightly more likely to be subject to strategic reasoning than the party vote. However, this result may simply be a consequence of the choice people are asked to make during an election rather than strategic considerations as such; in particular, one should not forget that the

---

8. For Italy only, the party sympathy question was not available in the 2001 survey, thus I use the PTV question asking voters the probability of endorsing each possible party. While it is clear that PTV is not measuring preferences perfectly it provides us the closest possible measure to party sympathy for the Italian case.

SMD ballot presents voters with a much more limited choice than the PR ballot. Moreover, I find strategic variables to have a conspicuous impact on the party vote too. This is perhaps a consequence of contamination effects under mixed rules (Cox and Schoppa 2002; Herron and Nishikawa 2001). Such a result is also consistent with the idea that the vote under PR rules is also subject to strategic incentives (Abramson et al. 2010; Blais et al. 2006). The result that small parties' supporters are more likely to change their mind during the electoral campaign tends to confirm that the proportional ballot too is subject to wasted vote considerations.

Overall, it seems that while the two votes are quite similar, party-level specific variables explain the party vote better than the candidate vote. Differently, the local context seems to play a larger role on the candidate vote when compared to the party vote. There are some interesting differences across countries according to the types of electoral rules as found already in the first step of the analysis. Overall, however, strategic considerations, if existing, are very low and similar in the two tiers of the ballot paper.[9]

Additional considerations

So far, the analysis has included five established democracies. Expanding the analysis to very different electoral contexts can be useful to generalise the results gathered so far. To this aim, this section uses data from the Comparative Study of Electoral Systems (CSES) on Albania, Hungary, Thailand and South Korea.[10] This extension is carried out with two caveats. For one, while for the previous sample of countries the independent variables are measured at using pre-electoral data and the dependent variable using post-electoral data, in this case I only dispose of post-electoral data, which means that all the variables are measured at time t. For another, for these countries, CSES does not make available, for each respondent, the district-level identifier. Consequently, I am unable to link each respondent to the district in which the vote is being cast and thus, I cannot include in multivariate models the following independent variables: Incumbency, DContention and Margin. The results of the analysis are shown in Table 4.4.

The first results from Table 4.4 show a clear no pattern across countries. Party identification is statistically significant for both votes in South Korea and Thailand but while it has a very similar impact on the two votes in South Korea

---

9. An analysis of respondents' responses confirms low level of strategic considerations indicating that both votes should be considered a sincere reflection of voter preferences. For instance, when Scottish voters were asked how did they cast the party and candidate vote respectively, the majority responded that they intended to vote for 'the best party' (48% and 49%), moderately fewer that they 'always vote that way' (22% and 21%). Very few, specifically about 5% and 3% in the PR and SMD vote respectively, claimed that 'It's my second preference; I vote for my first-preference party in the other vote' and finally roughly 6% and 7% claimed that 'I really preferred another party but it had no chance of winning in this region/constituency'.

10. Other mixed-member electoral systems for which CSES data exist cannot be included in this analysis, either because information on one of the two votes is missing or because information on part preferences is missing.

Table 4.4: Vote choice and its determinants: conditional logit models, sample II

	Albania (2005)		Hungary (1998–2002)		Thailand (2007)		South Korea (2004–2008)	
	VOTE PR	VOTE SMD	VOTE PR	VOTE SMD	VOTE PR	VOTE SMD	VOTE PR	VOTE SMD
Choice-specific								
PID	-0.45	-0.57*	0.02	-0.01	4.59***	2.25***	2.83***	2.29***
	(0.32)	(0.26)	(0.07)	(0.08)	(0.72)	(0.48)	(0.13)	(0.12)
Party Sympathy	0.40***	0.45***	0.44***	0.41***	0.97***	0.75***	0.11***	0.02
	(0.02)	(0.03)	(0.02)	(0.02)	(0.05)	(0.04)	(0.02)	(0.02)
Individual-specific								
	Ref: PD		Ref: MSZP		Ref: PPP		Ref: GNP	
	PS		Fidesz		DP		UDP	
Age	0.00	0.00	-0.01	-0.01	0.00	0.00	-0.01	0.01
	(0.00)	(0.01)	(0.01)	(0.01)	(0.00)	(0.00)	(0.01)	(0.01)
Education	1.19*	0.57	0.23	0.22	0.01	0.04	0.03	0.39
	(0.58)	(0.59)	(0.30)	(0.30)	(0.32)	(0.28)	(0.39)	(0.35)
Female	-0.09	0.00	0.26	0.34	0.10	0.01	0.14	0.04
	(0.15)	(0.15)	(0.21)	(0.21)	(0.06)	(0.05)	(0.08)	(0.07)
	PR		SZDSZ		CTP		LFP	
Age	0.00	0.00	0.02**	0.01	0.00	0.00	-0.02	0.00
	(0.00)	(0.01)	(0.01)	(0.01)	(0.01)	(0.00)	(0.01)	(0.01)
Education	1.63**	0.64	-1.34***	-1.45***	0.37	0.31	-0.19	-0.88
	(0.50)	(1.26)	(0.39)	(0.39)	(0.49)	(0.42)	(0.61)	(0.59)

(Continued)

Table 4.4: Vote choice and its determinants: conditional logit models, sample II (Continued)

	Albania (2005)		Hungary (1998–2002)		Thailand (2007)		South Korea (2004–2008)	
	VOTE PR	VOTE SMD	VOTE PR	VOTE SMD	VOTE PR	VOTE SMD	VOTE PR	VOTE SMD
Female	-0.38	-0.31	-0.37	-0.17	0.02	-0.11	0.07	0.04
	(0.23)	(0.68)	(0.24)	(0.24)	(0.10)	(0.11)	(0.13)	(0.11)
	PSD		MIEP		PP		PPGA	
Age	0.00	-0.02	-0.02**	-0.03**	0.01	0.00	0.04***	0.03*
	(0.01)	(0.03)	(0.01)	(0.01)	(0.01)	(0.01)	(0.01)	(0.01)
Education	2.41***	0.16	1.11**	0.95**	-0.35	-0.85	1.53**	1.00
	(0.69)	(1.36)	(0.36)	(0.35)	(0.75)	(0.75)	(0.49)	(0.55)
Female	-0.16	0.20	-0.03	0.20	-1.01*	-0.83	0.07	-0.02
	(0.21)	(0.31)	(0.26)	(0.26)	(0.45)	(0.49)	(0.11)	(0.12)
	LSI		FPP		RC		DLP	
Age	-0.01	-0.02	0.02***	0.01**	-0.01	-0.00	-0.01	-0.00
	(0.01)	(0.01)	(0.01)	(0.01)	(0.03)	(0.02)	(0.01)	(0.01)
Education	0.95	0.78	0.76**	0.65*	-0.71	-1.17	0.68	0.16
	(0.81)	(0.80)	(0.26)	(0.26)	(1.07)	(0.81)	(0.55)	(0.57)
Female	-0.92*	-0.58	0.46**	0.57**	-0.30	-1.04	-0.01	-0.38
	(0.41)	(0.40)	(0.18)	(0.18)	(0.73)	(0.99)	(0.14)	(0.35)
	PDR		MDNP					
Age	0.01	0.01*	0.00	0.00				
	(0.01)	(0.01)	(0.01)	(0.01)				

(Continued)

Table 4.4: Vote choice and its determinants: conditional logit models, sample II (Continued)

	Albania (2005)		Hungary (1998–2002)		Thailand (2007)		South Korea (2004–2008)	
	VOTE PR	VOTE SMD	VOTE PR	VOTE SMD	VOTE PR	VOTE SMD	VOTE PR	VOTE SMD
Education	13881	0.20	0.97*	0.77*				
	(0.75)	(0.92)	(0.41)	(0.38)				
Female	-1.75***	-1.30*	-0.30	0.07				
	(0.52)	(0.63)	(0.29)	(0.27)				
N	3546	3546	8058	8058	6335	6335	4420	4420
LL	-601.87	-329.62	-1462.89	-1532.36	-383.19	-503.92	-861.93	-853.90
AIC	1247.73	703.25	2969.77	3108.73	802.38	1043.83	1759.86	1743.81

Notes: Dependent variable is vote choice in the PR and SMD respectively. Source: see Appendix to this chapter. Key to parties: Albania: Democratic Party (PD), Socialist Party (PS), Republican Party (PR), Social Democratic Party (PSI), Socialist Movement for Integration (LSI), New Democratic Party (PDR); Hungary: Hungarian Socialist Party (MSZP), Alliance Young Democrats (Fidesz), Independent Smallholder Party (SZDSZ), Alliance of Free Democracy (MIEP), Hungarian Justice Party (FPP), Hungarian Workers Party (MDNP); Thailand: Palung Prachachon (PPP) People Power Party, Democrat Party (DP), Charthai Party (CTP) Thai Nation Party, Puea Pandin Party (PP) For the Motherland, Ruam Jai Thai Chart Pattana (RC); South Korea: Grand National Party (GNP), United Democratic Party (UDP), Liberal Forward Party (LFP), Pro–Park Geun-hye Alliance (PPGA), Democratic Labor Party (DLP). Estimations performed using the asclogit-command in Stata version 13. Standard errors in parentheses: *p<.05, **p<.01, ***p<.001. Additional note see Table 4.3.

it is much more important on the PR when compared to the SMD in Thailand. Long-term party identification is not important in Hungary while in Albania it has an interesting negative effect only on the SMD vote. Party sympathy has a positive effect across all countries generally and a higher impact on the PR than on the SMD vote, with an exception made for South Korea in which case the variable is only significant on the PR vote. Comparing the two samples of countries in Table 4.3 and Table 4.4, party identification plays a much lower role in newer democracies when compared to older democracies. In addition, the influence of the determinants of vote choice is much more similar across older democracies than across newer democracies. In any case, on the one hand, the results in Table 4.4 confirm that the two votes are indeed different: party-level variables are more important on the PR vote when compared to the SMD vote where parties appear less important to explain patterns of vote choice overall. On the other hand, strategic voting, if present, impacts the two votes almost equally.

Summary

This chapter used a cross-vote and a cross-country analysis to provide insights into two related issues. The first issue concerns how different the two votes are when it comes to sincere and strategic considerations. The second issue relates to the effect of institutional variation across countries using different mixed rules. To substantively investigate these two questions, the analysis took two methodological departures from the existing literature. First, intended and actual vote choice in the two parts of the electoral ballot have been considered with the aim to detect differences and similarities between the two votes. Second, actual vote choice in the two tiers of the electoral ballot have been analysed separately using the same sets of independent variables. Moreover the use of the stacked data file allowed an assessment of the impact of individual, party and aggregate-level features simultaneously.

Two broad conclusions are noteworthy. Concerning voters' sincerity, the analysis made it clear that voters do not see the world as black and white and they tend to use the two-ballot system to express a nuanced vote choice. Indeed the two votes appeared different in that parties' preferences matter in the PR much more than they do in the SMD vote. Conversely, the features of the local context weight more on the majoritarian tier when compared to the proportional tier. These differences notwithstanding, the analysis makes clear that strategic voters will act upon strategic incentives on both ballots and the vote under majoritarian rules is only slightly more likely to be impinged by strategic reasoning.

With regard to a comparison across countries, I find remarkable similarities across countries but also some interesting differences across types of mixed systems and level of experience with the electoral rules. Strategic coordination by voters appears clearer in mixed-proportional systems such as Germany and New Zealand which are also the countries that have used the systems for the longest period of time. Mixed-proportional systems also differ from mixed-majoritarian ones in that they provide less evidence of personal voting. When it comes to the group of newer democracies, the patterns of vote choice are quite heterogeneous across countries but overall it seems that parties impinge on voters overall much less than in more established democracies.

There are two issues left unclear from this chapter's discussion. First, because of the inclusion of several countries and since in the majority of these countries questions on candidate preferences are not available, the analysis has examined voting behaviour using exclusively individual-level information on parties' preferences. Information on how much voters like candidates has not been included because it was unavailable. The second issue is that the comparative analysis was unable to control for 'forced' split-ticket vote. This limitation stems from the fact that information on the district in which the candidate vote is cast is only available for about half of the countries analysed. Consequently, it was impossible to control whether voters had the same party available on both electoral ballots or if they were forced to split. These additional investigations are carried out in the next two chapters of this book using the national elections in Japan and the regional elections in Italy.

Chapter Five

Parties, Candidates and Forced Split-Ticket Voting: Evidence from Japan

A mixed-majoritarian system has been in use in Japan since the 1996 elections. As in all other mixed systems, Japanese voters cast two votes, one for a local candidate using majoritarian rules and one for a national party under proportional rules. Despite a great deal of research on the impact of the electoral reform on the Japanese system as a whole, less has been written about why Japanese voters split their ticket by voting simultaneously for a party and a candidate affiliated to another party. This is especially surprising given that the few existing works on ticket-splitting in Japan have shown that a significant number of voters split their vote, usually impacting on the overall electoral outcome (Reed 1999; Kabashima and Reed 2001; Burden 2009). The Japanese case is of particular interest for the analysis conducted in this book due to the type of electoral rules alongside the availability of extensive individual and aggregate-level data.

First, concerning its electoral rules, Japan represents the classical instance of mixed-majoritarian system diffused in several other countries as well, including some in Africa and East-Europe. However, the Japanese system is one of the oldest examples of mixed-majoritarian rules, thus providing this study with extensive evidence on the impact the electoral rules have on vote choice in general and split-ticket voting in particular. Second, the Japanese party system has been characterised by profound changes which, as discussed below, have evolved from a quasi-unique case of a one-party dominated system into a more common, multiparty system. Above all, the Japanese case provides rich data not available in other countries. In particular, the data in Japan allows for disentanglement of different types of split-ticket voting (sincere versus strategic) from accidental split-ticket voting. Studying the factors influencing ticket-splitting is possible using Japanese surveys as they contain questions about the rationale behind vote switching and thermometer questions about feelings for parties and candidates running for elections not limited to one year of election. Furthermore, it is possible to control for forced split-ticket voting, because information about the district in which the vote has been cast is readily available.

The analysis conducted in this chapter is relevant to Japanese politics, because it highlights causes and consequences of the mixed system electoral reform. At the same time, this study has a broader reach given the possibility in this context to analyse the impact on split-ticket voting of preferences for both parties and candidates simultaneously while controlling for the actual presence or absence of certain candidates on the ballot paper.

This chapter starts with a brief overview of the Japanese electoral setting and by outlining the theoretical expectations. Then, it provides an exploratory picture of split-ticket voting in Japan using aggregate data. Finally, survey data is analysed to answer questions concerning the possibility of different types of split-ticket voting and to determine whether or not decisions to split correlates with notions of rational vote maximisation. Concluding remarks close this chapter.

The Japanese case

Public demand for reform, the widespread support for change among members of the parliament and the formation of a coalition of government that 'agree on little else than the necessity of enacting reform' (Reed 2005: 280) made the transition from a Single Non-Transferable Vote (SNTV) system to a majoritarian mixed-member electoral system transpire in 1993. The new electoral system was introduced for both the lower (House of Representatives) and the upper house (House of Councillors) of the Japanese Parliament (Diet) for the first time during the 1996 election. In this chapter I focus exclusively on the lower house. Under these new electoral rules, voters elect 300 members of the lower house using single-member district (SMD) and 180 members using proportional rules (PR).

In terms of allocation of parliamentary seats, the two tiers of the ballot paper are completely separated. The unique seat in each SMD is allocated to the candidate who wins the majority of votes; seats in the PR tier are distributed among the parties using closed lists and the D'Hondt formula. The party vote is assigned at the 'block' levels as opposed to the national level, thereby limiting further the proportionality of the system by lowering the district magnitude. There are in total eleven PR blocks with district size ranging from six to thirty. When entering the polling place, Japanese voters receive two blank ballot papers. The first ballot is to be filled inside one of the SMD booths, where lists of candidates and their party affiliation is present. After they have voted, voters receive another blank ballot to be cast in one of the PR booths where the voter finds a list of the parties presenting candidates in that PR block (Reed 2005).

Before the electoral reform, the Japanese system consisted of one large party, the Liberal Democratic Party (LDP) dominating three or four smaller opposition parties that were never able to win control of the government. After the reform, Japanese politics entered a phase of fluidity with the proposal, and founding, of many new parties. Under the new electoral rules, the chances for smaller parties to obtain seats have slightly increased despite remaining generally significantly low (Reed 2003: 193). Although the LDP has survived to form a variety of coalitions ranging from a minority to an over-sized majority, the Democratic Party of Japan (DPJ) has continued to counter the LDP governments since 1998 (Kato and Kannon 2008).

Table 5.1 reports the national aggregate party and candidate vote for all major parties in Japan for each election since the introduction of the mixed system in 1996. The table indicates that the LDP usually performs better in the SMD than in the PR tier. For instance, the LDP received about 33 per cent of the total party vote, but almost 39 per cent of the candidate vote in 1996. Such difference across the two tiers increased over the following years reaching a maximum in 2012 when the difference between the party and the candidate vote for the LDP party exceeded 16 per cent. This finding is perhaps not surprising since the LDP is the only party, excluding the small Japanese Communist Party (JCP) in the 1996 and 2000 elections, which run candidates in the overwhelming majority of the SMD contexts. In other words, at the district level, the LDP likely receives additional candidate votes from supporters of those parties who do not run candidates. The trend between the party and the candidate vote is reversed for smaller parties; they usually perform better in their party vote than in the SMD vote. For the DPJ the trend is fluctuating across elections. However, the difference between the party and the candidate vote is much lower for the LDP.

Thus, these aggregate results suggest that a sizeable number of voters who voted for an LDP candidate on the SMD ballot selected a different party on the PR ballot. These patterns are consistent with an explanation that many supporters of smaller parties in the PR wanted to split supporting a LDP candidate on the SMD ballot. This result could also arise from voters being forced to split since the party supported on the proportional ballot does not run a candidate. One finding is clearly evident: the fact that almost the same percentage of people vote in the two tiers of the ballot paper (see last row of Table 5.1) indicates that split-ticket voting must be responsible for these patterns of voting.

Table 5.1: Percentage of votes won by parties in the two parts of the electoral ballot

	Party Vote						**Candidate Vote**					
	1996	*2000*	*2003*	*2005*	*2009*	*2012*	*1996*	*2000*	*2003*	*2005*	*2009*	*2012*
LDP	32.8	28.3	35.0	38.2	26.7	27.6	38.6	41.0	43.8	47.8	38.7	43.0
DPJ	16.1	25.2	37.4	31.0	42.4	16.0	10.6	27.6	36.7	36.4	47.4	22.8
JCP	13.1	11.2	7.8	7.3	7.0	6.1	12.6	12.1	8.1	7.3	4.2	7.9
SDP	6.4	9.4	5.1	5.5	4.3	2.4	2.2	3.8	2.9	1.5	2.0	0.8
NFP	28.0	–	–	–	–	–	28.0	–	–	–	–	–
CGP-Komeito	–	13.0	14.8	13.3	11.4	11.8	–	2.0	1.5	1.4	1.1	1.5
JRP	–	0.4	–	–	–	20.4	–	2.0	1.3	–	–	11.6
Others	18.2	12.9	0.0	4.7	8.2	15.7	8.0	13.5	7	5.9	6.6	12.4
Valid Votes	59.6	62.5	59.8	67.5	69.3	59.3	59.6	62.5	59.9	67.5	69.3	59.3

Notes: Key to parties: LDP – Liberal Democratic Party; DPJ – Democratic Party of Japan; JCP – Japanese Communist Party; SDP – Social Democratic Party; CGP – Komeito-Clean Government Party; Conservatives Party; NFP – New Frontier Party; JRP – Japan Restoration Party.

Source: http://www.electionresources.org/jp (accessed 3 July 2013).

Existing literature

Given the prevalence of split-ticket voting in Japanese elections, it is surprising that relatively few studies have investigated the event in detail. Using the candidate vote gap data, measured as the difference between the vote for the party and the linked candidate at the district level, Reed (1999) found a conspicuous amount of voters deserting candidates unlikely to win the single-member district seats. The author also found a strong correlation between positive candidate vote gaps and a candidate's chances of winning the single-member district seats. This finding led Reed to claim support for the wasted vote strategic hypothesis in the 1996 Japanese elections. Using data at the prefecture level for the 1996 elections, Kohno (1997) draws similar conclusions. As extensively discussed in Chapter Three of this book, the empirical evidence from aggregate-data is limited as these differences say little about when and where the switching occurs. This limitation stems from the fact that aggregate calculus are likely to underestimate levels of split-ticket voting as they cannot account for all the cross-voting among parties and candidates in the two parts of the electoral ballot. Importantly, the observed aggregate patterns of vote choice are compatible with multiple explanations at the individual level; indeed the exclusive use of aggregate data does not allow us to disentangle sincere from strategic motivations.

In fact, voters can cast a split in a sincere fashion. Firstly, voters may have contrasting feelings for parties and candidates running for elections (Gallagher 1998: 209); voters are more likely to split when the most preferred candidate belongs to a different party than their preferred one. The legacy of the previous system, the features of the new electoral system and the characteristics of Japan's party politics all suggest the presence of high levels of personal voting in Japan. Specifically, the now-defunct SNTV system played an important part in exacerbating the highly personalistic nature of the Japanese political system (Reed 2003). In addition, many features of the new Japanese mixed system can create incentives for personalistic politics. For instance, the dual candidacy feature, on the basis of which parties can run the same candidate on both ballots, reinforces the candidates' personalistic campaign to attract personal voting on both tiers (McKean and Scheiner 2000). Furthermore, it has been highlighted that the lack of linkage between the two tiers provides parties with strong incentives to focus on taking as many SMDs as possible by encouraging their own candidates to seek personal votes (Moser and Scheiner 2004, 2005). The availability of strong LDP candidates well known at the municipal level and their persistence on the ballot paper tends to reinforce these patterns (Reed 2003; Burden 2009). Relying on aggregate data only and the vote gap measure, Moser and Scheiner (2005) found that patterns in the 2000 elections in Japan look more consistent with personal vote for candidates rather than strategic voting. This result has been confirmed in the 2000 election by Burden (2009) using aggregate and individual-level data. Overall, failing to control for candidate preferences is likely to overestimate the impact of strategic considerations.

Similarly, not all voters find the party that they supported on the PR to be available on the SMD ballot, so they may be forced to split their vote due to limited choice on candidate tier. The existing literature does not explore this feature of forced voting mainly as the analysis is rather complex for two reasons. First, information on the local district where the candidate vote has been cast is not always available. Consequently, in these cases, it is simply not possible for researchers to know whether or not the party for which the people voted also ran a candidate. Second, even when information on the district is available, modelling voting preferences with regard to forced voters is not straightforward. This difficulty stems from voters being forced to split; for this reason, they cannot be included in common models of split-ticket voting where the dependent variable is a dummy measuring the probability of splitting the ticket. Hence, more often than not, forced voters are excluded from the analysis. Excluding forced voters means assuming that they would have cast a straight vote if it were possible. This assumption is questionable since we know that many non-forced voters split their ticket anyway. On the other hand, the lack of consideration of the issue assumes that all voter preferences are available on the electoral ballot, possibly overestimating the effect of voter preferences and motivations. The analysis conducted in this chapter addresses this issue by examining separately forced and non-forced voters.

Hypotheses and operationalisation

The focus of the following analysis is to disentangle three types of split-ticket voting that at both individual and aggregate-level generate identical patterns. These types are: 1) sincere, 2) strategic and 3) forced ticket-splitting.

Starting with sincere voting, first, in the case of voters who identify with a party or who strongly prefer a party above all the others, parties can function as the principal voting cue (Campbell and Miller 1957). For this reason, I hypothesise that these voters will be more likely to 'simply' cast a straight vote for the party they identify with the most or that they prefer the most among all the other parties. The effect of a strong commitment to a party can be investigated examining the classical question, 'Do you usually think of yourself as close to any political party?'. I expect that party identifiers will be more likely to cast a straight vote than non-identifiers (*Party identification hypothesis*).

While party identification represents a long-term commitment to a party, party sympathy based on the question 'How much do you like party X using a scale from 0 to 10 where "0" means "I don't like the party or the candidate at all" and "10" means "like the party or the candidate very much"?' is intended to capture more short-term oscillation (e.g., Converse and Pierce 1986: 339). This question provides an indication of how much utility a voter can expect to receive from his support for each party. One expects that the more the respondent likes the party, the less likely the voter should be to cast a split vote (*Party sympathy hypothesis*). The same question asked for parties is available for candidates; specifically, respondents have been asked thermometer feeling questions for all candidates running for election in the respondent's district. The expectation is that the more the respondent likes the candidate, the less likely the voter should be to cast a split-ticket vote (*Candidate sympathy hypothesis*).

The feeling thermometer questions can also be used to construct a measure that takes into account how much the voter likes the best party (candidate) when compared to all the others. The best party (candidate) is the party (candidate) scored highest by the respondent on a scale from 0 to 10. Some voters may only like a single party (candidate) whereas other voters may score multiple parties (candidates) equally, or nearly equally high (Marsh 2006*b*). Consequently, voters who like more than one party (candidate) similarly will be more likely to split their vote than those who have a strong commitment to one party (candidate) above all the others (*Party or Candidate ties hypothesis*).

There are other ways to measure the influence of personal voting in addition to candidate sympathy. The standard method is to employ incumbency as performed in current analyses of split-ticket voting. The expectation is that incumbent candidates via their personality and visibility will increase straight vote and decrease split-ticket voting for their own parties (*Incumbency hypothesis*). However, the use of incumbency to capture personal vote is problematic as it cannot disentangle strategic motivations from more sincere ones. For instance, when supporters of small parties, such as the JCP, defect from the party's candidate by voting for an LDP candidate, this defection may be strategic as well as due to the personal features of the LDP candidate. Fortunately, surveys in Japan allow me to use not only incumbency, but also more direct information on familiarity and feelings for candidates. In particular, I employ a candidate knowledge variable capturing to what extent the voter knows the candidate using the question 'How well do you know the [named] candidate?' with options, 'no knowledge', 'know somewhat' and 'know the candidate very well' (*Candidate knowledge hypothesis*).

Moving to strategic considerations on the SMD ballot, candidate spending has been used by the existing literature as a measure of candidate viability: indeed, above all, candidate spending by parties is aimed to convince voters that the candidate has a good chance of winning the SMD race (Johnston and Pattie 2000). Several studies, particularly in New Zealand, use party spending to show that more spending by parties in the SMD increases parties' ability to retain majoritarian votes (Johnston and Pattie 2000; Karp *et al.* 2002). The expectation is that the more the party spends on its candidate, the less likely a voter should be to split the ticket (*Candidate spending hypothesis*). However, in Japan, a candidate's spending is strongly correlated with a candidate's vote share given that incumbent candidates tend to spend much more than challenger candidates (Cox and Thies 2000). Thus, I also use an interaction term in the models below between spending and incumbent status.

When it comes to strategic voting on the PR, supporters of big parties can strategically split on the PR vote after casting a sincere candidate vote in order to favour the least-worst option and to help this party cross the electoral threshold. In the Japanese case, the low 2 per cent threshold may not induce bigger parties to cast a strategic PR vote for a small party (Gallagher 1998: 209), but the reverse can take place. Since the 2003 elections, parties frequently enter into formal pre-electoral coalitions in many districts by presenting common candidates. This occurs, for instance, in the case of the LDP and the junior coalition partner Clean Government Party (the Komeito) (CGP-Komeito). The presence of these firm alliances between parties and their coordination in some of the SMD districts, may induce supporters of one party to support another party when the preferred one is not available in line with a possible coalition outcome. Thus, I control for coalition preferences; the hypothesis is that voters are more likely to split when they have a preference for a coalition government rather than for a single-party government (*Coalition preference hypothesis*). The variable I built takes a value of one if the respondent prefers a coalition rather than a single-party government and that party is included in the preferred coalition government and 0 otherwise.

Evidence from aggregate-level data

This chapter looks at aggregate data first to provide an exploratory analysis and then it moves to individual-level data to confirm or reject the substantive conclusions reached using aggregate results. For each pair of graphs displayed below, each graph on the left, plots values of the candidate vote gap as calculated by subtracting from the candidate vote the total vote for the party in each district. Positive values indicate that the candidate did better than her own party whereas a negative gap means that the party outperformed the candidate. Each graph on the right displays the values of ticket-splitting by the candidate at the SMD level as calculated using the Multinomial-Dirichlet method (Rosen *et al.* 2001).[1]

Starting with Figure 5.1, the plot on the left shows that patterns of candidate vote gap are similar across elections, following a unimodal distribution with a mode just above zero, which means that on average candidates slightly outperform parties. The explanation for this is quite simple: since in most districts voters were offered more PR than SMD choices, unless a differential in turnout takes place, the votes for candidates will generally be higher than those for parties. This measure is limited by several methodological flaws, because the differences between SMD and PR vote for each party hide all the cross-voting among parties and candidates. For example, if ten LDP supporters vote for a DPJ candidate and ten DPJ voters vote for a LDP candidate, the aggregate figure will return no party defection for both parties and a zero vote gap. For this reason, I also consider estimates of split-ticket voting. The plot on the right of Figure 5.1 indicates that aggregate patterns of split-ticket voting are quite stable across elections with the 2005 election resembling to some extent an outlier. The shapes of the distributions are due to the fact that large parties are characterised by very low levels of split-ticket voting (mode around zero) whereas very small parties show high levels

---

1.   Recall that this method has been assessed to be the best performing method among the ones tested in Chapter Three of this book and this is the reason why this chapter relies on the Rosen *et al.* (2001) method exclusively.

Figure 5.1: Candidate vote gap and split-ticket voting (%), overall

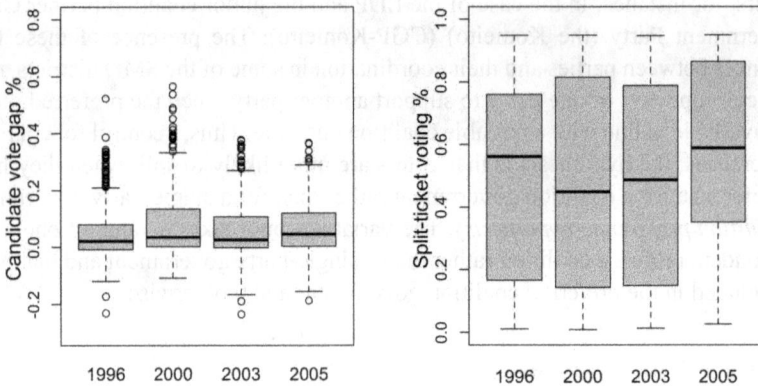

Notes: The figure plots quantities by party at the SMD level. Estimated values use the Multinomial-Dirichlet method (Rosen *et al.*, 2001).

Source: Candidate Vote Gap: own elaboration from data provided by Asano and Yanai (2013). Estimations: were performed by me using municipality level data provided by Jun Saito.

of ticket-splitting (mode around one). The third mode, around the middle of the distribution (5 per cent), is increasingly visible starting from the 2000 election onwards and becoming much clearer during the 2005 election.[2]

Figure 5.2 provides the same quantities as Figure 5.1 but it presents them as a function of party share of vote with distinct colours and shapes enabling us to differentiate across parties. The x-axis of the previous figure is now the y-axis, and the horizontal axis plots values of party share of votes. The plot on the left of Figure 5.2 shows a scatter plot with a weak but visible positive relationship between the candidate vote gap and the party vote. This result indicates that the bigger the party, the better its candidate performs in each district. Despite this result, however, the funnel shape towards higher values of the party vote indicates that a few big party candidates are characterised by negative vote gaps and perform worse than some smaller parties' candidates, such as JCP and NFP. CGP-Komeito is the only party featuring consistently positive gaps. This finding is not surprising given that the CGP-Komeito regularly coordinates with the LDP and only runs candidates in districts where the LDP does not endorse candidates. The results are to some extent confirmed by looking at the plot on the right in Figure 5.2, which shows that the LDP and the DPJ are characterised by the lowest levels of split-ticket voting with a few exceptions. There is, however, a great deal of variability in the levels of split-ticket voting.

---

2. This third mode represents the parties, such as the DPJ and the JCP, which run candidates also in some of the districts where they have no chance of winning. This issue will be discussed more extensively in the following sections.

Figure 5.2: Candidate vote gap and split-ticket voting (%), by party

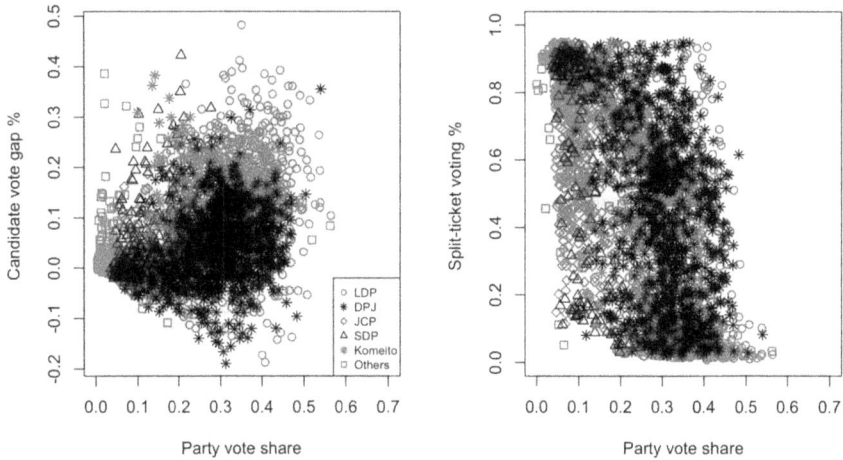

Notes: Key to parties see Table 5.1. For additional notes see Figure 5.1.

Figure 5.3 and Figure 5.4 show the same quantities but as a function of incumbency status and candidate spending respectively. First, Figure 5.3 clearly illustrates that incumbent candidates are those who feature high percentages of candidate vote gap and low levels of split-ticket voting. Challenger candidates

Figure 5.3: Candidate vote gap and split-ticket voting (%), by incumbency status

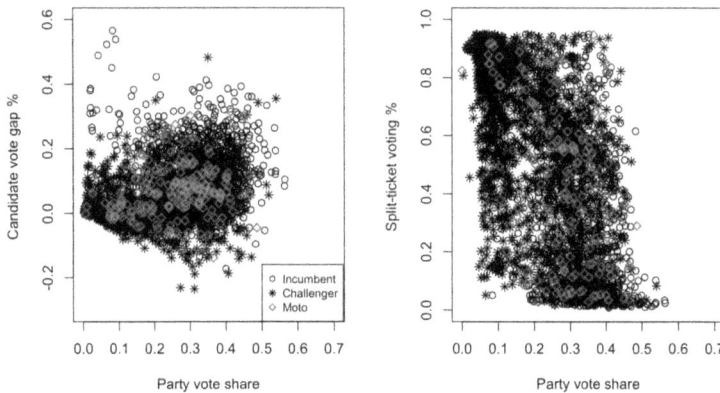

Notes: 'Incumbent' and 'Challenger' mean respectively that a candidate has won or not won the SMD district during the previous election. 'Moto' means that the candidate was a member of the parliament in the past but not an incumbent in the current election. Additional notes see Figure 5.1.

Figure 5.4: Candidate vote gap and split-ticket voting (%), by category of spending

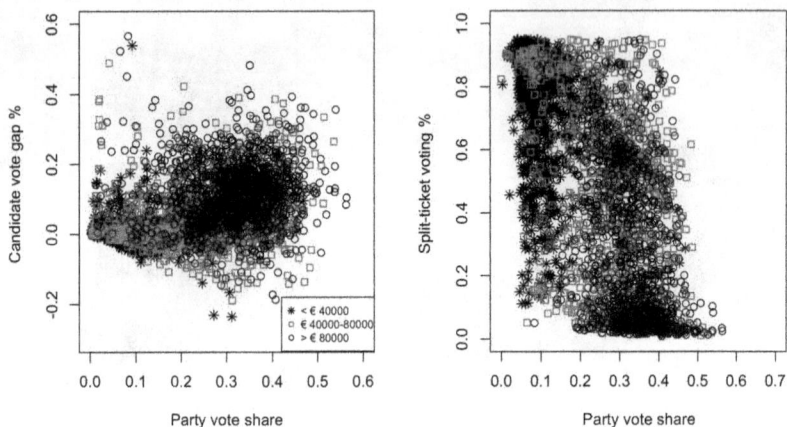

Notes: Candidate spending figures from 1996 onwards were provided by Asano and Yanai (2013).

show an almost opposite pattern whereby 'moto' candidates, those who were members of the parliament but not incumbent in the current election, position themselves at half way. Finally, Figure 5.4 reports the candidate vote gap and estimates of split-ticket voting by share of party vote and by category of spending. Clearly, the more a candidate spends, the more likely they are to gain more votes than her own party and lower levels of split-ticket voting. The largest variability in terms of split-ticket voting is to be observed at moderate values of spending by candidates.

To sum up, bigger parties' candidates receive larger vote gaps and lower levels of split-ticket voting than smaller parties' candidates. At the same time, incumbency and candidate spending are positively correlated with the vote gap and negatively correlated with split-ticket voting. Clearly, aggregate results are consistent with a strategic argument and in line with current studies findings. The next section clarifies the meaning of these patterns by focusing directly on voters' preferences and motivations.

Evidence from individual-level data

As stated in the outset of this chapter, Japanese surveys are useful to analyse types of split-ticket voting since they contain questions about the rationale behind vote switching; at the same time they enable us to control for forced split-ticket voting. The focus of the following analysis is to disentangle three types of split-ticket voting that at the both individual and aggregate-level generate identical patterns. These types are: sincere, strategic and forced ticket-splitting.

Explorative patterns

In the 1996 pre-electoral context, when Japanese voters were asked about the expected outcome of the election in relation to their SMD vote,[3] an overweening majority (70 per cent) picked the option that the candidate for whom they intended to vote for 'will definitely or probably win' the elections; less than 20 per cent said that the candidate 'will win with a small margin', about 9 per cent said 'probably won't win' and just below 2 per cent said that the candidate 'will definitely lose.' When asked a similar question in 2003 and 2005 pre-electoral surveys, roughly the same percentages can be found, a result that indicates that the majority of the respondents think, correctly or not, that the candidate they intend to vote for will certainly or probably win the SMD elections.

Furthermore, respondents who had the intention to support a different party on the two ballots, that is to split their vote, were asked why. An analysis of the responses to this question suggests that almost 40 per cent of voters can be regarded as forced splitters (they picked the option 'there is no candidate from the party that I support'); at least 24 per cent of the split vote is to be considered sincere (voters picked one of the following options: 'in the PR there is a candidate that is not from the party I support for whom I would like to vote' or 'I choose for whom to vote regardless of the candidate's affiliated parties'). Just above 8 per cent can be considered strategic according to the wasted vote hypothesis (voters picked one of the options: 'the candidate from the party I support will certainly win even if I do not vote for him/her' or 'the candidate from the party I support will certainly lose') and a percentage of about 12 per cent can instead be considered strategic according to the coalition voting hypothesis having picked the option 'I consider the balance of the seats in the House'.

Regarding personal vote, in 1996 respondents were asked if they cast the candidate vote based more on the party or more on the candidate. Roughly 41 per cent chose the option 'more on party', about 46 per cent 'more on candidate' with the rest choosing the 'both' option. In 1996 under the new electoral system, only the LDP and the JCP were running under the same party labels as they had in 1993, so this result is surprising. When asked the reason for choosing the party on the PR, nearly 23 per cent picked the option because they 'favoured candidates on the PR list', but about three times more (above 65 per cent) said because of the 'party's policies', because they 'liked the party' or because they have 'been voting for the party before.' In the post-electoral survey for the 2003 and 2005 elections, when Japanese respondents were asked which factors did they consider when voting, more than 30 per cent in the SMD and about 40 per cent in the PR said because they supported the party. Similar percentages have been reported for all the other options except for the option 'because of the personality of the candidate', which has been chosen by 20 per cent of the respondents in the SMD and only 5 per cent for the PR,

---

3. The question employed in the 1996 survey is: 'Do you think the candidate you intend to vote for will win the election?'

and the option 'because of the party policy', which has been chosen by only 9 per cent of respondents in the SMD and 19 per cent in the PR vote. Broadly speaking, this pattern of responses is a sign that vote choice is 'party-centred' rather than 'candidate-centred'. Despite this, however, the features of the candidates matter a good deal especially on the SMD ballot. It is possible to analyse this further by investigating whether ticket-splitting is a result of multiple preferences for more than one party or candidate using feeling thermometer questions.

I first check the following: do straight voters rank the party and the candidate voted for differently than splitters? The answer is yes; straight voters rank the party or the candidate voted much higher than the other parties or candidates; for splitters the difference of rating between the top ranked party and the others is much smaller. The second question deals with straight voters by asking: do straight voters show differences in the way they rank the party and the candidate they voted for? The answer is no; straight voters rank the party they voted very similarly to the candidate and specifically at least two percentage points higher than the other parties or candidates. How about splitters? Do they rank parties and candidates differently?

The answer is yes; in the case of splitters it makes a big difference whether one examines the rating for the party or the one for the candidate voted. First and foremost, overall candidate rating explains the candidate vote better than the party vote and vice versa. Looking at the party vote, splitters vote for the party they ranked highest; at the same time, however, voters do not always rank highest the candidate's party for which they have voted. For instance, those who voted for a CGP-Komeito candidate ranked the LDP party highest, those voting for a SDP candidate, ranked the DPJ party highest. Thus many votes for a candidate come from supporters of other parties. This can be a sign that voters follow parties' suggestions on how to cast their SMD vote. For instance, there is clear indication that among those rating LDP highest, many have voted for a CGP-Komeito candidate thus clearly following LDP party instructions.

Many split votes can come about because the most preferred candidate does not run linked to the preferred party. As a matter of fact, examining candidates rating alone, those voting for a candidate usually rated that candidate highest. Quite on the contrary, examining the rating of the candidates starting from the party vote, often voters did not rank the party's candidate highest. This suggests the presence of a conspicuous amount of misalignment between preferences for parties and candidates. For instance, CGP-Komeito party supporters rank LDP candidates almost as high as the candidate from the CGP-Komeito party. In some extreme cases, such as for DPJ, LDP candidates are rated even higher than DPJ ones. This result suggests that many voters like candidates not belonging to their most preferred party, and LDP candidates are usually among the most liked ones.

To sum up, exploratory findings using surveys suggest that straight-ticket voters have stronger feelings for parties than splitters and they remain loyal to their party on both votes. Splitters, on the other hand, generally have a weak party attachment, but not too weak and they will cast their vote based on other motivations. Apparently, what really determines the type of vote cast is how much a voter likes a party when compared to all the others. There appears to be some strategic coordination among smaller parties but contrasting feelings for candidates and parties appear to explain a great deal of the variation. A multivariate analysis will confirm these findings.

A multivariate analysis of split-ticket voting

The standard approach to the study of split-ticket voting utilises a dependent variable that measures the probability of casting a split rather than a straight vote. The dependent variable is a dummy taking a value of 0 every time the respondent casts a straight vote and 1 otherwise. I start the multivariate analysis relying on this model. Table 5.2 shows two logit model specifications (party-centred and candidate-centred) using pooled data for the 1996, 2000, 2003 and 2005 Japanese elections.[4] In the party-centred model, all the variables are built as usually done in the existing literature; that is as if the vote in mixed systems is party-centred. This means that all the variables are measured considering the party vote as it comes first; the voter is defined as a supporter of that party, whose vote choice on the majoritarian ballot can then be analysed to see if the voter follows that party or not. For instance, with reference to the first variable 'Party Identification' this is set at 1 if the respondent identifies with the party voted on the PR and 0 otherwise. On the contrary, in the case of the candidate-centred model, party attachment as well as all the other variables, are measured on the basis of the candidate vote; in this case, for instance, the Party Identification variable takes a value of 1 if the respondent identifies with the party of the candidate supported on the SMD. It is straightforward to see that for straight voters only, the variables in the two models' specification will be identical because the party on the PR coincides with the one supported on the SMD. The comparison of the two models allows me to check whether or not voters consider the two votes similarly while checking to what extent the current literature specification of the independent variable would provide different results than an alternative specification centred on candidates instead.

By definition, when one wants to measure the effect of the features of the candidate of the party voted for on the probability of splitting the ticket, when the party did not run a candidate on the SMD tier then that observation is lost in the regression models. Consequently, columns for Models 1 and 2 report the denomination of 'non-forced voters'. For the candidate-centred voters instead, one can include all observations because the independent variables are measured using the information on the candidate.

---

4. I run different model specifications by clustering errors by district and years of election or both and by running multi-level logit models. Different model specifications provide very similar results and do not affect the sign or significance of the coefficients. For this reason, I only present simple logit models with robust standard errors. I also tried to include a variable controlling for party size at the district level. The party size variable, however, showed high levels of correlation with spending and cannot be included in the final models.

Table 5.2: Explaining party defection: logistic regression

	Party-centred		Candidate-centred			
	Non-forced		Non-forced		All voters	
	(Model 1)	(Model 2)	(Model 3)	(Model 4)	(Model 5)	(Model 6)
PID	−0.604***	−0.606***	−1.273***	−1.276***	−1.403***	−1.403***
	(0.149)	(0.149)	(0.154)	(0.154)	(0.110)	(0.110)
Party sympathy	−0.080*	−0.072	−0.144***	−0.143***	−0.052*	−0.052*
	(0.040)	(0.040)	(0.036)	(0.036)	(0.025)	(0.025)
Party ties	0.248	0.247	0.308*	0.303*	0.205*	0.205*
	(0.139)	(0.140)	(0.130)	(0.130)	(0.101)	(0.101)
Candidate sympathy	−0.281***	−0.280***	−0.052	−0.051	−0.073**	−0.073**
	(0.027)	(0.027)	(0.029)	(0.029)	(0.022)	(0.022)
Candidate ties	0.022	0.044	0.025	0.034	−0.066	−0.066
	(0.161)	(0.162)	(0.158)	(0.158)	(0.125)	(0.125)
Candidate knowledge	−0.394***	−0.448***	0.028	0.014	−0.156**	−0.155**
	(0.093)	(0.095)	(0.078)	(0.079)	(0.057)	(0.057)
Incumbency	−0.507***	−1.481***	−0.020	−0.353	−0.007	−0.027
	(0.127)	(0.305)	(0.125)	(0.292)	(0.093)	(0.217)
Candidate spending (€ 1000)	−0.002	−0.007**	−0.000	−0.003	−0.001	−0.001
	(0.002)	(0.002)	(0.002)	(0.002)	(0.001)	(0.002)
Incumbency X Candidate spending (€ 1000)		0.012***		0.004		0.000
		(0.003)		(0.003)		(0.002)
Coalition preference	0.027	0.027	−0.029	−0.030	0.152	0.153
	(0.122)	(0.123)	(0.116)	(0.117)	(0.087)	(0.087)
Gender	−0.119	−0.107	−0.062	−0.063	0.062	0.062
	(0.123)	(0.124)	(0.117)	(0.117)	(0.086)	(0.086)
Age	−0.003	−0.003	−0.012**	−0.011**	−0.010***	−0.010***
	(0.004)	(0.004)	(0.004)	(0.004)	(0.003)	(0.003)
Education	0.146	0.143	0.271**	0.270**	0.141*	0.141*
	(0.097)	(0.097)	(0.091)	(0.091)	(0.067)	(0.067)
Constant	1.042*	1.369**	0.148	0.304	0.413	0.422
	(0.408)	(0.419)	(0.386)	(0.405)	(0.288)	(0.304)

(Continued)

Table 5.2: Explaining party defection: logistic regression (Continued)

| | Party-centred | | Candidate-centred | | | |
| | Non-forced | | Non-forced | | All voters | |
	(Model 1)	(Model 2)	(Model 3)	(Model 4)	(Model 5)	(Model 6)
N	2698	2698	2698	2698	3143	3143
Pseudo-R2	0.144	0.150	0.081	0.082	0.082	0.082
Nagelkerke-R2	0.198	0.205	0.115	0.116	0.131	0.131
LL	−930.86	−924.55	−1004.14	−1003.34	−1659.59	−1659.59
AIC	1.887.71	1.877.10	2.034.28	2.034.68	3.345.19	3.347.18

Notes: Standard errors shown in parentheses *p < 0.05, **p < 0.01, ***p < 0.001.

Source: Surveys for all elections are provided by the Social Science Japan Data Archive, The University of Tokyo. Spending figures were provided by Asano and Yanai (2013).

I focus first on the models without interaction terms (Models 1, 3 and 5). In the hypotheses section, I listed several arguments which refer broadly to parties, candidates and district-level features. Starting with parties, Table 5.2 indicates that having a party attachment reduces the probability of observing a split vote. The effect is negative and statistically significant across all models but stronger for the candidate-centred models. With regard to the party sympathy, one expects that the more the respondent likes the party or the party's candidate for whom she voted for on the PR, the less likely the voter should be to cast a split vote. The empirical findings support these expectations. However, the effect is again stronger for the candidate-centred models when compared to the party-centred models. I also expect that voters who like more than one party similarly will be more likely to split their vote than those who have a strong commitment to one party above all the others. The Party Ties variable is positive across all models but statistically not significant only for the candidate-centred models.

Moving from parties to candidates, the sympathy score variable is negative as expected. On the other hand, having warm feelings for more than one candidate does not appear to have an effect on the probability of splitting the ticket. This finding suggests that defection is not based on how much a voter likes his party's candidate when compared to the other candidates but rather on how much she likes her party when compared to the other parties as well on how much the voter likes their own party's candidate. With regard to candidate knowledge, this variable has a negative significant impact on split-ticket voting as hypothesised but its effect is not statistically significant in Model 3.[5] Similarly, running an incumbent

---

5. An analysis across years of election shows that the effect of this variable decreases over time, being quite strong in 1996 and increasingly lower in subsequent elections. This finding is in line with the existing literature expectations suggesting that despite the fact that electoral outcomes in Japan will continue to be influenced by voters' evaluations of the candidate, this feature should lessen as parties become increasingly institutionalised (Reed 2003).

decreases the probability of splitting as others have previously found (e.g., Burden 2009). However, the variable is statistically significant only in the party-centred models. With regard to party spending on candidates, the expectation is that the more the party spends on its candidate, the less likely a voter should be to split the ticket. Table 5.2 shows that on a general level spending is negative but generally not statistically significant. The models also control for coalition preferences. Model 1 in Table 5.2 shows that coalition preferences have no impact on split-ticket voting. I also control for socio-demographic variables, such as education, age and gender. While education has a positive and significant effect on split-ticket voting, all the other demographic variables are insignificant.

Given the correlation between candidates' spending and candidates' vote share, I control for candidates' spending and simultaneously assess the relationship between spending and incumbency.[6] The interaction effect results are presented in Model 2, Model 4 and Model 6: the interaction term is positive and statistically significant but only in the party-centred model. As the interpretation of logistic regression coefficients and interaction terms in particular are notoriously difficult, I graphically show the results of this interaction. Figure 5.5 displays the marginal effect of incumbency by candidate spending based on Model 2 and Model 4 respectively. The graph shows the substantive moderating effect of incumbency, which increases the predicted probability of splitting the vote by about 5 per cent indicated by the upward trend in the marginal effect of incumbency. The effect is, however, statistically significant only for relative low levels of candidate spending: increasing levels of spending are much more rewarding for challengers than for incumbents but this holds true only for lower levels of spending. On the other hand, spending by candidates makes almost no difference in the case of candidate-centred voters. Several studies in the US (e.g., Abramowitz 1991; Jacobson 1990) and elsewhere (e.g., Palda and Palda 1998; Carty and Eagles 1999; Johnston and Pattie 2006) have found comparable results (see also Benoit and Marsh 2008).

To sum up, party attachment and party feelings reduce the probability of observing a split vote even more for the candidate-centred when compared to the party-centred models. Conversely, the variables measuring candidate preferences that I found having generally a negative impact on split-ticket voting in party-centred models are less important in the candidate-centred models. Similarly, running an incumbent is statistically significant only in the party-centred models. Thus, it seems that to explain a split in the SMD vote both parties and candidates are important; on the other hand, a split on the PR is almost exclusively explained looking at parties. In other words, after choosing the most preferred candidate on the SMD, only how much voters like the affiliated party matters. Contrarily, after picking the best party on the PR, how much a voter likes a party and a candidate

6.   A deeper inspection shows that spending is highly correlated also with the competitiveness of the district race. Candidates tend to spend much more in more competitive districts while official spending is lower in safer districts confirming a standard finding in studies in US and elsewhere (e.g., Stratmann 2005).

Figure 5.5: Campaign spending effect moderated by incumbency status

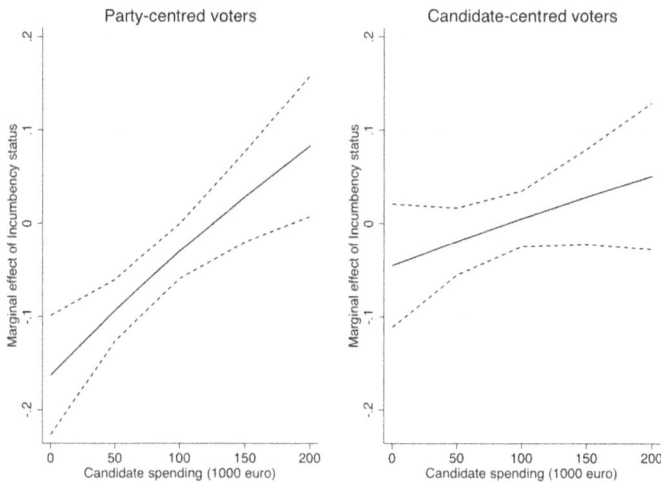

to decide if she will split or not are important. Three main findings can be derived from the analysis. For one, it is clear that both party and candidate features are important determinants of split-ticket voting. The addition of candidate-centred variables brings down the effect of parties as well as more strategic considerations such as those related to coalition preferences and candidate spending. Additionally, the analysis shows that measuring the split starting from parties or candidates has an effect on substantive conclusions and as such the findings from the existing literature provides only a limited view of the phenomenon. Finally, it is clear that the two votes, the PR and the SMD vote, are cast somewhat differently by voters. But how much different are the two votes? And particularly, how differently do forced voters behave?

A comparative view of the two votes

As mentioned in the outset of this chapter, many voters may not have had any choice but to split given that smaller parties do not run candidates in many SMDs. Modelling forced voters represents a big challenge for scholars of split-ticket voting. This challenge stems from the fact that forced voters show no variation on the standard dependent variable measuring the probability of splitting the ticket. Consequently, current analyses focus primarily on non-forced voters and/or disregard completely the matter. This section adds to the knowledge of split-ticket voting by expanding the analysis to forced voters. The focus is to investigate how different the two votes are and whether or not forced voters behave differently from non-forced voters. To conduct such analysis, I employ survey data using 'stacked' datasets in a way similar to what has been done in Chapter Four. In this context, the dependent variable is a dummy taking a value of 1 each time the respondent voted for party X (or candidate X) and 0 otherwise. Concerning the independent variables, they refer to all parties and candidates running for elections.

When the party did not run a candidate, the row corresponding to that candidate contains missing values. This missing data are not truly missing but simply do not exist. Excluding all these values means analysing only those cases where all parties and candidates run for elections reducing the sample to non-forced voters again. For cases in which the missing values do not exist, Allison (2001) suggests plugging in some arbitrary value for all missing data cases and then include in the regression a dummy variable coded 1 if data in the original variable are missing and '0' otherwise. Following Cohen and Cohen (1975), Allison (2001) explains that while this 'dummy variable adjustment' is clearly unacceptable when data are truly missing (e.g., respondents refuse to answer a question in the survey for instance), it may still be appropriate in cases where the unobserved values simply do not exist.[7] I follow this argument in the analysis below. Table 5.3 shows the results.

First of all, the results are unsurprisingly similar between the 'All Voters' and the 'Non-forced' models, because non-forced voters represent the majority of all voters. Starting with the Party Vote, parties matter slightly less for non-forced voters than for all voters; at the same time, candidates matter more. It is important to note that the variable Incumbency and candidate spending are positive and statistically significant only in the case of non forced-voters. Moving to the Candidate Vote, parties matter more for forced voters than for non-forced voters; at the same time, candidates matter just a little bit more for the first group of voters. In other words, when voters are forced to split their vote, candidate features, and incumbency, in particular, appear to matter much more than when they are not forced. Put simply, there are two remarks one can draw from this analysis. The first remark is that when voters are non-forced, the features of the candidate and the party affect the other vote more than when voters are not forced; equivalently this means that contamination effects between the two tiers are clearly visible. On the other hand, when voters are forced, candidates' parties' affiliation remains important to explain the candidate vote. Coalition preferences are quite important and explain the two votes almost equally well.

Skimming through the party-level results, individual level socio-demographics features have a different effect across parties, but also across voters. Additionally, they are generally more important in the party vote, which overall appears to be more easily predicted by these long term individual-level features. The two votes are indeed different: the features of the party explain the party vote better than the candidate vote and vice versa for the candidate vote. The vote still looks

---

7. Suppose one assumes that there is one linear equation for non-forced voters and another equation for forced voters. The non-forced equation is identical to the forced equation except that it has (a) a term corresponding to the effect of candidate features on the dependent variable and (b) a different intercept. Allison (2001) explains that it is easy to show that the dummy variable adjustment method produces optimal estimates in this situation.

Table 5.3: A comparison of the two votes: conditional logistic regression

	VOTE PR		VOTE SMD		
	All voters	*Non-forced*	*All voters*	*Non-forced*	*Forced*
	(Model 1)	(Model 2)	(Model 3)	(Model 4)	(Model 5)
PID	0.821***	0.793***	0.640***	0.743***	0.235
	(0.075)	(0.090)	(0.087)	(0.094)	(0.279)
Party sympathy	0.446***	0.426***	0.281***	0.325***	0.141**
	(0.019)	(0.023)	(0.019)	(0.022)	(0.047)
Candidate sympathy	0.237***	0.304***	0.525***	0.534***	0.509***
	(0.022)	(0.026)	(0.028)	(0.031)	(0.076)
Candidate knowledge	0.056	0.109	0.083	0.105	0.006
	(0.049)	(0.059)	(0.057)	(0.063)	(0.171)
Incumbency	0.054	0.188**	0.353***	0.307***	0.549**
	(0.056)	(0.063)	(0.059)	(0.064)	(0.172)
Candidate spending (€ 1000)	−0.001	−0.003***	−0.004***	−0.004***	−0.006**
	(0.001)	(0.001)	(0.001)	(0.001)	(0.002)
Coalition preference	0.951***	1.169***	0.929***	0.915***	0.992***
	(0.078)	(0.098)	(0.088)	(0.097)	(0.230)
dummy	0.536***	0.161	0.374*	0.627***	−0.649
	(0.134)	(0.158)	(0.163)	(0.181)	(0.445)
Ref: LDP					
DPJ					
Gender	−0.327***	−0.288**	−0.064	−0.073	0.281
	(0.099)	(0.108)	(0.106)	(0.114)	(0.326)
Age	−0.009*	−0.008*	−0.002	−0.006	0.024*
	(0.003)	(0.004)	(0.004)	(0.004)	(0.011)
Education	−0.112	−0.119	0.001	−0.055	0.295
	(0.076)	(0.084)	(0.081)	(0.087)	(0.266)
Constant	0.671**	0.588*	−0.125	0.232	−2.650***
	(0.228)	(0.252)	(0.241)	(0.263)	(0.755)

(Continued)

Table 5.3: A comparison of the two votes: conditional logistic regression (Continued)

	VOTE PR		VOTE SMD		
	All voters	*Non-forced*	*All voters*	*Non-forced*	*Forced*
	(Model 1)	(Model 2)	(Model 3)	(Model 4)	(Model 5)
CGP					
Female	0.230	0.389*	0.419*	0.660***	−0.366
	(0.124)	(0.188)	(0.168)	(0.190)	(0.422)
Age	−0.006	−0.011	0.003	0.000	0.017
	(0.004)	(0.006)	(0.006)	(0.006)	(0.014)
Education	0.254*	0.555***	0.523***	0.531***	0.439
	(0.099)	(0.150)	(0.132)	(0.150)	(0.339)
Constant	−0.209	−1.104**	−1.686***	−1.629***	−2.201*
	(0.280)	(0.424)	(0.379)	(0.434)	(0.865)
SDP					
Female	−0.038	−0.126	0.150	0.210	−0.105
	(0.180)	(0.283)	(0.244)	(0.265)	(0.698)
Age	0.002	−0.013	−0.010	−0.009	−0.010
	(0.006)	(0.009)	(0.008)	(0.009)	(0.022)
Education	0.511***	0.176	0.386*	0.443*	0.029
	(0.134)	(0.213)	(0.180)	(0.194)	(0.559)
Constant	−1.551***	−1.274*	−1.416**	−1.476**	−1.507
	(0.409)	(0.596)	(0.507)	(0.571)	−1.142
JCP					
Female	−0.187	−0.149	0.203	0.237	0.169
	(0.174)	(0.183)	(0.177)	(0.196)	(0.448)
Age	−0.006	−0.007	−0.004	−0.006	−0.002
	(0.006)	(0.006)	(0.006)	(0.007)	(0.015)
Education	0.492***	0.534***	0.384**	0.358*	0.479
	(0.128)	(0.134)	(0.132)	(0.146)	(0.338)
Constant	−0.969*	−0.849*	−1.241**	−1.114*	−1.734
	(0.384)	(0.410)	(0.393)	(0.441)	(0.900)
N	18735	16245	18735	16245	2490
LL	−3254.12	−2204.36	−2412.52	−2047.15	−307.70
AIC	6.556.23	4.456.72	4.873.05	4.142.31	663.40

Notes: Dependent variable is vote choice in the PR and SMD respectively. Key to parties: Liberal Democratic Party (LDP), Democratic Party of Japan (DPJ), Komeino-Clean Government Party (CGP), Social Democratic Party (SDP), Japanese Communist Party (JCP). Estimations performed using the asclogit-command in Stata version 13. Standard errors in parentheses:*p<.05, **p<.01, ***p<.001.

Source: see Table 5.2.

party-centred when voters have a party identification; candidates' features, on the other hand, explain the two votes better when voters have no party attachment. When it comes to forced voters, despite the fact that for these voters party features matter less, it is clear that parties continue to influence vote choice on both ballots. In answering the question, would forced voters have cast a straight vote if their candidate or party was available on the electoral ballot or would they have split anyway, the results suggest that their choice will depend on how much they like the party but not on how much they like the affiliated candidate.

Summary

Much has been written about the impact of the 1994 electoral reform on Japanese politics. Little focus has been devoted to voting behaviour under the new two-vote system and much less has been written about split-ticket voting. This is surprising if one considers that the few existing works have shown that in Japan a significant number of people split their vote and this group of voters has a significant impact on the electoral outcome (Reed 1999; Kabashima and Reed 2001; Burden 2009). More often than not, the current Japanese literature on split-ticket voting examines the candidate vote gap to discuss the performance of parties and candidates in the two electoral ballots. Despite the candidate vote gap in the SMD being a consequence of split-ticket voting, its use will not help us in disentangling the reasons why people split. Furthermore, aggregate patterns that suggest strategic voters' reaction to the electoral offer are entirely consistent with at least two other types of individual-level rationales. Wider vote gaps in the SMD for bigger parties can indeed indicate personal voting or forced split-ticket voting.

The aggregate-level evidence from this chapter suggests that patterns of split-ticket voting are consistent with a strategic explanation. Estimations show that big parties are characterised by higher levels of defection than those suggested by crude aggregate measures. Despite this, however, estimation results remain consistent with a strategic argument and in line with current studies findings. Conversely, the analysis of surveys reveals that what appears to be strategic is instead the result of sincere preferences for a party and a candidate that just happens to run for another party. There is clear evidence that the two votes are cast differently by voters with features of the party explaining the party vote better than the candidate vote and vice versa for the candidate vote confirming findings from Chapter Four of this book. The investigation identifies the presence of two groups of voters: party-centred voters usually with a strong party identification, and those who value candidates more. For forced voters, party features still matter the most but the candidate vote looks much more candidate-centred. The disentanglement of the different types of split-ticket voting suggests that the limited candidate menu restricts voter's choice but many voters would have probably switched party on the SMD tier anyway. Overall, split-ticket voting in Japan is strategic only in those few cases where it is not a consequence of personal voting and it is not forced.

The findings presented in this chapter are relevant to Japanese politics and beyond. With regard to Japan, the analysis suggests that the mixed-majoritarian system in use is surely not the 'best of both worlds' (Shugart and Wattenberg 2003) for small parties that are characterised by high levels of splitting and will rarely beat strong party candidates in the majoritarian race. If small parties want to win the SMD seat, they will need to coordinate with bigger parties. Coordination seems to work with many voters following parties' instructions and by splitting the ticket in a way consistent with formal pre-electoral agreements. On the other hand, the mixed system appears to be good for voters who, being able to vote for both a party and a candidate, are free to express a nuanced electoral choice. The analysis conducted in this study has broader implications. Findings show that ticket-splitting is a consequence of a multitude of factors which depends only in part on the electoral rules and strategic incentives. The disentanglement of these factors, however, is only possible when pre- and post-electoral survey data ask questions about all parties and candidates running for elections. Fortunately, these questions are increasingly present in national election studies. Future research on split-ticket voting and the interconnectedness between parties and voters' strategic actions should point their attention to those questions to uncover the causes of split-ticket voting avoiding unnecessary assumptions about voter sincerity that often, such as in this case, prove to be quite inaccurate.

Chapter Six

Pre-Electoral Coalitions and Split-Ticket Voting: Evidence from the Italian Regional Elections

This chapter employs the regional elections in Italy to further expand the study of split-ticket voting. The Italian case is of particular interest for this book due to its unique mixed rules as well all the significant regional differences it exhibits. With regard to the electoral system, the Italian regional system is the only instance of mixed rules where pre-electoral coalition agreements are displayed on the electoral ballot. To be sure, in many mixed-member electoral systems there is a widespread practice of parties to run common candidates on the SMD ballot while still running as independent entities on the PR ballot. Thus, in almost all mixed systems the candidate menu is always a restricted version of the proportional ballot and voters are often instructed on how to behave when their party's candidate is not available. However, the Italian case represents the unique case where pre-electoral cartel arrangements are displayed on the ballot paper. This means that voters can be straight- or split-party voters when their party is available on both ballots; when not available, voters can be straight- or split-coalition voters. This possibility allows for interesting considerations and it offers insight into the widespread practice of presenting voters with pre-electoral coalitions in many mixed systems. Here I investigate specifically the extent to which, and under what circumstances, elite coordination on the SMD is effective in preventing voters splitting to other coalitions.

When it comes to the regional variation, two features are of particular importance for the study conducted in this book. For one, the Italian mixed system is peculiar in that it allows for variation of the mixed electoral rules across sub-national units. For this reason, even if all the regions must maintain a mixed system they can alter it by, for instance, increasing the electoral threshold. These additional features permit an original investigation not possible in any other country where, during the same election, the electoral rules remain constant across sub-national units. For another, Italy's electoral behaviour has always been very geographical with different voting traditions across macro regions of the country (Cartocci 1990; Agnew 2002; Diamanti 2003). By leveraging on the estimation procedures discussed in Chapter Three, it is possible to assess the effect of macro foundations of voting like long-term party loyalties and socio-demographics characteristics on split-ticket voting while investigating the effect of the electoral rules and cartel arrangements.

This chapter starts with a brief overview of the Italian case. It then introduces the data and measurement and it continues by outlying the theoretical expectations. Subsequently, the chapter describes the results based on the use of aggregate data. Finally, the chapter discusses the results and their implications.

The Italian regional case

In Italy there are three levels of sub-national government: 20 regions (*regioni*), 107 provinces (*province*) and about 8100 municipalities (*comuni*). The Constitution divides the Italian regions into two groups, namely, 'ordinary' and 'special' where the main difference regards their relative power and independence from the central state. The 15 ordinary regions which this analysis focuses on are: in the North: Piemonte, Lombardia, Liguria, Friugli-Venezia Giulia and Veneto; in the Centre: Emilia-Romagna, Toscana, Umbria and Marche and in the South: Lazio, Molise, Campania, Puglia, Basilicata and Calabria. The three groups of regions have, in the past, been characterised by distinct voting traditions due to the social and institutional differences among the North, the Centre and the South of the country (e.g., Putnam 1993; Pasquino 1995). When considering the most recent years, it is still possible to isolate these three homogenous electoral areas in Italy also in regard to the Italian regional elections. Whereas the Centre of the country is strongly leftist, the other areas are subject to more political competition with the North being slightly more rightist recently (Agnew 2002; Diamanti 2003).

A rather complex mixed system was introduced in Italy in 1995 (D'Alimonte 2005: 273; Di Virgilio 2005). Under the Italian regional electoral system voters have two votes: they choose by proportional rules a party list at the provincial level, with the second vote they choose by plurality a list at the regional level connected to a candidate for the presidency of the region. The proportional vote is cast using open-lists with a threshold of 3 per cent, unless the party is connected to a presidential candidate, which obtains more than 5 per cent of the vote, in which case the threshold for the single party is only 1.5 per cent (also known as 'double-threshold' mechanism) (Di Virgilio 2002). Thus, 80 per cent of the seats are assigned on the proportional tier, in addition the winning regional list on the majoritarian tier will receive a bonus of 20 per cent (or more) – enough to ensure a majority of at least 55 per cent of the seats in the regional council.[1] From 1999 onwards modifications are possible on the basic mixed-member electoral systems introduced in 1995 and each region can adopt slightly different electoral rules while maintaining the basic mixed system. Only few regions have used this opportunity, mostly starting from 2005. The changes concern, for instance, the allocation of the majority seat bonus, the provision of gender quotas in the party lists, rules of intra-party competition and modifications of the electoral threshold (e.g., Floridia 2005; Pacini 2007).

As it happens in other mixed systems, coordination efforts of parties on the majoritarian tier have been increasingly common. Since the introduction of the new electoral rules, parties have increasingly coordinated by presenting common symbols and forming pre-electoral coalitions on the majoritarian tier, while still running as independent entities on the proportional tier (Di Virgilio 2007). The electoral ballot usually displays two large pre-electoral coalitions, the centre-left and the centre-right, each endorsed by one of the two largest Italian parties plus

---

1.   D'Alimonte (2005) also labels this system as a 'majority assuring system' or 'a direct election of the prime minister system'.

several junior coalition allies (Appendix 6.I provides an example of the ballot paper). The two largest parties today are: on the left, Partito Democratico (PD), up until 2007 named Democratici di Sinistra (DS) and before 1998 named Partito Democratico della Sinistra (PDS); on the right, Il Popolo della Libertà (PdL) formed in 2009 by the fusion between Forza Italia (FI) and Alleanza Nazionale (AN). Beside the two largest pre-electoral coalitions, there are several smaller ones generally endorsed by smaller parties. Party systems and pre-electoral coalitions differ from one region to another while they are the same across districts of the same region; only the composition of the pre-electoral coalitions, e.g. the number of coalition partners, may slightly change from one district to another within the same region.

Italian voters have two options. They can follow their party into the coalition by casting a straight vote or they can split the vote by supporting a different coalition than the one that their party indicated to coalesce with. As the electoral rules allow for the formation of pre-electoral coalitions, only one party for each coalition will present its own candidate and thus, several parties' supporters will be 'frustrated' (Benoit *et al.* 2006) because their candidate is not running. Given that a voter prefers a party nominating its own candidate and another voter prefers a party with a candidate of an allying coalition, a straight-ticket vote does not have an identical meaning to both voters. As explained below, the presence on the ballot paper of the parties' candidate should and will be empirically controlled for. Voters can also abstain in one part of the ballot by supporting only a party or a coalition/candidate.[2]

The dependent variable

At the aggregate level there are two ways of examining vote choice in this rather complex context; both need to take into account that under the Italian regional electoral rules the vote for a pre-electoral coalition on the majoritarian tier is also a vote for a candidate. The first way is by measuring the 'coalition vote gap' calculated as the vote difference between the votes gained by the coalition/candidate and the parties endorsing that coalition/candidate at the district level.

---

2. The analysis conducted in this chapter is concerned with those voters who cast both votes however, because casting only one vote may still be related to the research question discussed in this chapter, the analysis needs to take this into account. Ideally, one would want to know how many voters only cast one vote. Knowing how many only voted for parties is impossible because under the Italian electoral law, the party vote is automatically counted also for the linked coalition/candidate. However, the reverse is not true: a vote for a coalition/candidate is only counted on the majoritarian tier. One way of gauging the 'only-majoritarian' vote is by calculating aggregate differences between the two tiers. These values are discussed in the chapter under the name of vote gap and, as explained, they suffer from the ecological fallacy problem. A second way to measure the only-majoritarian vote is by using ecological inference estimation. Estimations obtained using the Rosen *et al.* (2001) method show that the only-majoritarian vote is generally below 5 per cent of the total party vote cast at the provincial level. These low values indicate that while some coalitions/candidates do receive more votes than the parties linked to them, the overwhelmingly majority of voters cast both votes.

The vote gap is a measure of how much the coalition/candidate outperforms the linked parties. Positive values indicate that the coalition/candidate did better than the parties, whereas a negative gap means that the parties outperformed the coalition/candidate.

As already discussed in Chapter Three of this book, the vote gap measure is problematic but especially so in the Italian context. First, these differences mask cross-voting among the two tiers of the electoral ballot, a problem known as the 'ecological fallacy' (Robinson 1950). Second, official electoral results only report the total vote for the coalition/candidate and the vote for each party. Consequently, it is only possible to measure the vote gap at the coalition-level and no information is available at the party level. Due to the limitations of the vote gap measure, this chapter also considers estimates of the vote patterns obtained using the Rosen *et al.* (2001) method, which in Chapter Three of this book, has been shown to be the best performing among the methods tested.[3] The Rosen *et al.* (2001) method uses Bayesian statistics to estimate intra- and inter-coalition flows of voting employing aggregate electoral results. The lowest level of aggregation for which electoral data is available for the Italian regional elections is the precinct level (*comune*).[4]

---

3. In addition, I statically compare the results of the Rosen *et al.* (2001), the Greiner and Quinn (2009) and the Goodman's (1953) method using the Root Mean Squared Error (Root-MSE). Root-MSE ranges from 0 to 1 where '0' means that values estimated using one method are identical to the values estimated by a second method; conversely, larger values of Root-MSE indicate more divergent results. The analysis indicates that values of the Root-MSE are generally quite small, which means that the results do not greatly differ across methods. Specifically the Root-MSE between Rosen *et al.* and the Greiner and Quinn is 0.31; between the Rosen *et al.* and the Goodman it is 0.38 and between the Greiner and Quinn and the Goodman it is 0.38. Other scholars have found comparable results when testing how different findings are when using older versions of these methods (e.g., De Sio [2009]).

4. It is true that whenever possible, one should carry out the estimations using data at the lowest level of aggregation, which - in our case - is the polling station level (sezione elettorale) (e.g., De Sio 2009). I have not done so because data for the Italian regional elections are only available at the next upper level of aggregation (*comune*). This can constitute a limitation to our analysis given that data at the municipality level may not be sufficiently homogeneous. To address this issue I run a specific test. The standard error associated with the estimates provides information on the 'quality' of the estimate. Broadly speaking, when the standard error is very large this is a sign that the estimate is of low quality, which should be related, among other things, to the problem of non-homogeneity just mentioned. It is then possible to exclude all the estimates associated with a standard error above an established threshold from subsequent multivariate models. I found that about 5 per cent of our estimates can be regarded as problematic cases. I thus ran the multivariate models presented in the chapter again by including and then excluding these problematic cases. Since the results were no different in any important respect I have not included them in the chapter. In any event, as suggested by the methodological literature (e.g., Adolph *et al.* 2003), our multivariate models use WLS in which observations (estimates) are weighted by the inverse of the estimates' standard error as provided by the Rosen *et al.* (2001) method, thus giving greater weight to observations with more precise estimates. This means that problematic estimates with larger standard errors "weigh" less in the final results than estimates with smaller standard errors. Importantly, the fact that I can confirm aggregate level results by using individual-level data (see Appendix 6.II) indicates that the substantive conclusions reached in the chapter do not depend on the method or data used.

In summary, the two measures, vote gap and split-ticket voting, capture different phenomena. In the words of D'Alimonte (2001), it is possible to separate the 'gluing' effect, when the coalition/candidate is able to retain voters on the majoritarian tier (lower split-ticket voting), and the 'magnetic' effect, when the coalition/candidate is able to attract more votes than the linked parties (higher vote gap). Both measures, the vote gap and ecological inference estimates, are obtained using official electoral results available from the Italian Ministry of Interior website (www.elezionistorico.interno.it). The units of analysis for the vote gap are coalitions at the provincial district level. For split-ticket voting, the units of analysis are parties at the provincial district level. The analysis covers the four elections (1995-2010) held in the 'ordinary' region under mixed rules.

An extension of the aggregate-level analysis is carried out in Appendix 6.II using surveys. To this end, the analysis of split-ticket voting is replicated using a post-election telephone study conducted by Ipsos following the regional election in 2010. The use of surveys extends the evidence found using aggregate data by including also individual-level determinants. Even though a direct comparison between aggregate and individual level data should be done with caution, as the aggregate level analysis uses pooled data and the surveys only cover the 2010 election, the use of individual-level data, using the same independent variables while changing the level of investigation from the party to the individual can still provide a test for the aggregate-level findings presented in this chapter.

Expectations, hypotheses and operationalisation

Parties and candidates

I note first that when party elites decide to form a pre-electoral coalition, voters subsequently have two options: they could follow their preferred party's elites and stay within the coalition, or voters could desert the pre-electoral coalition to which their party belongs and cast their vote for some other party or coalition. For those who identify with a party, or strongly prefer a party above all the others, parties function as the principal voting cue (Campbell and Miller 1957). For this reason it makes sense to hypothesise that those voters will be more likely to 'simply' follow their party into the coalition, thus casting a straight vote. The effect of a strong commitment to a party can be investigated at the individual level as well as at the aggregate level. In the first case, it is possible to use the traditional question, 'Do you usually think of yourself as close to any political party?', and expect that identifiers will be more likely to cast a straight vote than non-identifiers (*Party identification hypothesis*).

The effect of partisanship can also be investigated at the aggregate level allowing room for contextual voting patterns. In the Italian context, party choice has been historically linked to specific areas of the country. Voters' affiliation, identification with parties and socialisation are indeed not transitory but represent a proper recognition in collective identities and the territorial context, which still proves important in explaining the Italian political behaviour (Bellucci and Segatti

2011). Centre-left parties have been traditionally very strong in the central regions of the country. The same holds true for the centre-right parties in the northern and southern regions, albeit to a lesser extent (Corbetta *et al.* 1988; Agnew 2002; Bellucci and Segatti 2011). Thus, one expects lower levels of vote gaps, and lower levels of split-ticket voting for specific political parties in those regions where they have been historically strong (*Party stronghold hypothesis*). The stronghold variable takes a value of one for a specific coalition when it has never lost an election across the four elections under investigation in this chapter.[5]

Yet, several conditions exist under which voters may deviate from these baseline predictions. The first hypothesis is based on the influence that candidates might have. Several scholars have proven that voters' evaluations of the personalities of candidates play an increasingly important role in determining electoral preferences (Shugart *et al.* 2005). Thus, the hypothesis is that when voters prefer a candidate that is nominated by a different party or coalition, they face serious cross-pressures to desert the pre-electoral coalition to which their party belongs to vote for that preferred candidate. Conversely, when the preferred candidate belongs to the coalition endorsed by the preferred party, this might serve as an incentive to remain loyal to the coalition. To assess the impact of candidates, this chapter gives attention to their key features, such as incumbency and being a nationally visible politician. The expectation is that high-profile candidates (via their personalities, media visibility and so forth) are more likely to increase the coalition/candidate vote share, and decrease split-ticket voting, than other candidates (*Incumbent and Party leader hypotheses*).

When discussing the effect of candidates it is important to consider the actual presence of the party's candidate on the ballot paper. Each coalition is formed by one candidate and at least one party but in most cases there are several parties endorsing one candidate. I defined as 'frustrated' the voters who prefer a party that is endorsing another party's candidate on the majoritarian tier of the ballot paper. It is reasonable to expect that frustrated voters will be more likely to split their vote than voters who are non-frustrated. At the district level, the presence of the candidate on the majoritarian tier is controlled for by building a variable, which takes a value of 1 when the party did not run its own candidate and 0 otherwise (*Frustrated party hypothesis*). At the individual-level, a variable is built to control whether the party supported by the voter on the proportional tier has run its own candidate or not (*Frustrated voter hypothesis*). Employing the same logic, an increase in ticket-splitting and lower vote gaps are expected where there are fewer candidates running, thus I control for the number of candidates running on the majoritarian ballot. Overall, I expect candidate-centred voting to increase the vote gap and decrease split-ticket voting.

---

5.   Thus, for the centre-right coalition, the stronghold variable takes a value of '1' in Lombardia and Veneto; for the centre-left coalition it takes a value of '1' in Emilia-Romagna, Toscana, Marche, Umbria and Basilicata.

Strategic voting

Previous chapters of this book have discussed the classical formulation of strategic voting under mixed systems, often called the 'wasted vote' hypothesis: voters are more likely to deviate from a straight vote when their party's candidate has no chance of winning on the majoritarian tier (Bawn 1999; Karp *et al.* 2002). A more recent strand of research has looked at another strategic hypothesis, yet in line with a split-ticket voting, often defined as 'coalition insurance' hypothesis (Gschwend 2007; Pappi and Thurner 2002; Shikano *et al.* 2009). Both hypotheses are based on the assumption that parties and candidates are available on the electoral ballot and the voters decide to desert them on the basis of strategic calculations. However, elite coordination may anticipate voter-level strategic coordination by forming pre-electoral coalitions on the majoritarian tier, which ultimately aims at conserving resources to expend on candidates who can actually win.

In Italy, formal coordination efforts on the majoritarian tier, together with the double-threshold mechanism, should strongly encourage voters to cast a straight vote providing them with no incentive to split strategically following either one of the two mentioned strategies, i.e. the wasted vote or coalition insurance hypothesis. With regard to party coordination on the majoritarian tier, Gschwend and Hooghe (2008: 560) explain that instrumentally motivated voters will understand the considerable benefits of joining a pre-electoral coalition. Thus if voters are instrumentally motivated and looking for ways to optimise the effect of their vote (Cox 1997), it seems likely that they will stay within the coalition. In addition, the double-threshold mechanism previously mentioned (on the basis of which parties are subject to an electoral threshold of 3 per cent – unless the party is connected to a coalition/candidate that obtains more than 5 per cent of the vote, in which case the threshold for the single party is only 1.5 per cent), reduces strategic incentives to a minimum; even if voters prefer a different coalition/candidate than the one endorsed by the party voted for, it makes little sense for them to split because this would reduce the opportunity of their party getting seats (Di Giovine and Pizzetti 1996). Put simply, via the double-threshold mechanism, the more votes there are for the allying coalition/ candidate, the higher the chances that the preferred party will need just 1.5 per cent of vote rather than 3 per cent to receive seats. Thus based on expectations of the election outcome, voters should cast a straight vote even when they prefer a different coalition/candidate.

When measuring strategic voting at the individual level, and based on the idea that highly educated and sophisticated voters are more likely to 'respond' to strategic incentives (e.g., Karp 2006), it makes sense to expect that these voters (via education or political interest) will be more likely to cast a straight vote than their least aware counterparts (*Voter sophistication hypothesis*). The literature on strategic voting has also considered aggregate district-level features supposedly correlated with a strategic reaction to the electoral rules (e.g., Niemi *et al.* 1992). Specifically for mixed systems, Moser and Scheiner (2005) suggest that the relationship between straight vote and competitiveness of the district race should help differentiate between strategic and personal voting for candidates. In the Italian context the mechanism is as follows, in the next paragraph.

When the district race is competitive because the vote difference between the two-top ranked coalitions/candidates is low, voters of the parties linked to the two top-ranked coalitions/candidates should cast a straight vote even when they prefer a different candidate. That is, since the two top-ranked coalitions/candidates are at risk of losing the majoritarian election by just a few votes, supporters of the constituent parties should vote for them casting a straight ticket. On the other hand, more split-ticket voting in competitive races means that the higher the risk for the coalition/candidate losing the election, the more likely people are to switch and vote for another coalition/candidate. This result would make no sense from a strategic point of view, and it is more easily interpreted considering, for instance, the presence of a strong candidate on the electoral ballot (which, when endorsed by another pre-electoral coalition, decreases the likelihood of a straight vote). Of course this non-strategic straight vote can come about for other reasons, such as protest voting; despite this however, the effect of candidate-specific factors is arguably the most important. For lowest-ranked coalitions/candidates the matter is more complicated: if a more competitive race should encourage a lower degree of straight votes to help the victory of the least-worst option among the two top-ranked coalitions/candidates, at the same time, less straight votes can be entirely consistent with personal voting (Moser and Scheiner 2005: 263) (*District competitiveness hypothesis*).[6]

To sum up, when people vote for their preferred party and the coalition/candidate that this party indicated to coalesce with, i.e. straight vote, this behaviour is consistent with both a party-centred choice and strategic voting. If the vote is party-centred then we should observe variables such as party identification and party stronghold decreasing the vote gap and increasing straight-ticket voting. Alternatively, if strategic voting exists, voter sophistication at the individual-level as well as district-level variables should have an effect on voting choice. Specifically they should decrease vote gap and increase straight-ticket voting.

Pre-electoral coalitions

Following the work conducted by Gschwend and Hooghe (2008), there are at least three factors related to pre-electoral coalition features that may have an impact on split-ticket voting. To distinguish the specific effect of pre-electoral coalition

---

6.   To differentiate between the impact of the competitiveness of the district race on candidates, interaction terms with district competitiveness are used. As explained by Moser and Scheiner (2005) by using interaction terms one avoids selection bias problems that would follow from attempting to test the same hypotheses by dividing the sample into only top-ranked candidates and only lower-ranked candidates. Also in this chapter, the mean-difference or 'centring' method of adjusting the interaction variables is employed. This method gives greater substantive meaning to the results for the dummy variables used to create the interaction terms.

agreements I include indicators of the quality of such agreements (ideological congruence and coalition experience) which should decrease the vote gap and split-ticket voting.

The most straightforward is ideological similarity: voters are not likely to vote for the sponsored coalition of the party they otherwise support if they expect that there will be too many policy concessions to make. Golder (2006) shows that the successful formation of a pre-electoral coalition is largely dependent upon the ideological distance between the coalition partners. Gschwend and Hooghe (2008) show that a similar logic is relevant for voters too. A result echoed by Debus and Müller (2014) who find that voters favour coalition governments with a low degree of internal programmatic heterogeneity. Consequently, the more congruent the ideological positions of the coalition partners, the more likely it is that supporters of the constituent parties will support the coalition at the polls. Considering the lack of information on the policy positions of parties at the Italian regional level, ideological similarity is empirically controlled using a variable which takes a value of 1 when the pre-electoral coalition does not include extremist parties and 0 otherwise. In addition, I consider whether or not the coalition underwent controversial discussion before the elections (*Policy-congruent coalition hypothesis*). For instance, with regard to the 2010 election, in those regions where the Unione di Centro, a centre-right party, joined the centre-left coalition provoking a split of other left-wing coalition allies, the centre-left coalition has been identified as a non-congruent coalition.

The size of the coalition partners is, however, a crucial element. While small parties' supporters should understand the considerable benefits of joining a pre-electoral coalition, they are also expected to defect more easily. It can be assumed that the larger coalition partners will, to a considerable extent, be able to impose their views on the junior coalition partners (see also Martin and Vanberg 2003). This means that junior coalition partners will face a difficult task in incorporating their views into the joint platform and, for supporters of these small partners, there are, therefore, fewer reasons to feel represented by the manifesto of the cartel (Gschwend and Hooghe 2008). The defection of small parties' supporters can come about for other reasons as well (e.g., protest vote). *In any case, the expectation is that supporters of smaller coalition partners more easily defect than supporters of the major coalition parties.* This argument finds support in the experimental study by Gschwend and Hooghe (2008). (*Small party hypothesis*).

It can be argued that time also plays a role in determining the responses of voters. The formation of a pre-electoral coalition implies that voters, to some extent, are required to re-adjust their mental map of the political space according to clues provided by the party elites (see also Kabashima and Reed 2001). The likelihood of voters following their party into a coalition should increase as the time elapsed since the establishment of the pre-electoral coalition increases (*Coalition experience hypothesis*). In the Italian case a dummy variable is built which takes a value of 1 when the parties run for the same coalition in the previous election-year and 0 otherwise.[7]

Significant regional variation

From 1999 onwards modifications are possible on the basic mixed-member electoral systems introduced in 1995 and each region can adopt slightly different electoral rules while maintaining the basic mixed system. In 2005, a few regions adopted modifications to the electoral rules: the changes concern for instance, the allocation of the majority seat bonus, the provision of gender quotas in the party lists, rules of intra-party competition and modifications of the electoral threshold (e.g., Floridia 2005; Pacini 2007). In particular, a change in the electoral threshold may bear consequences on vote choice that could affect the amount of vote gaps and split-ticket voting. The electoral threshold was modified in 2005 in Calabria, Puglia, Toscana and Campania. In the first three instances, the double threshold mechanism is no longer in place and the new electoral threshold of 4 per cent applies to all parties regardless of their coalition affiliation. Campania has instead eliminated the 1.5 per cent additional threshold.[8] Everything else being constant, a higher (lower) electoral threshold at the party level is expected to decrease (increase) the level of ticket-splitting by increasing (decreasing) the incentives for voters to vote strategically (*Electoral threshold hypothesis*). To examine the effects of these modifications a dummy variable is built which takes a value of 1 in those regions that have increased the electoral threshold and 0 otherwise.

Findings

Figure 6.1 shows values of the coalition vote gap on the left and split-ticket on the right. As mentioned, the vote gap is measured as the percentage difference between the votes gained by the coalition/candidate and those obtained by the linked party/parties at the provincial district level (on the total of each coalition vote). Figure 6.1 shows that the values of the vote gap are often quite small and that these values are rarely negative: this means that in the majority of cases, coalitions/candidates outperform the linked parties obtaining more votes than the party linked to them (positive vote gaps) and rarely the parties outperform coalitions/candidates (negative vote gaps). The only discernible pattern is the

---

7. Note that voters might have developed an independent preference order for a coalition that might not reflect the one of the parties; consequently they could also split their ticket sincerely. Studies of vote choice in Italy explain that certain centre-left voters have been developing a sort of 'coalition identity' (e.g., D'Alimonte and Bartolini 1998; Chiaramonte and D'Alimonte 2000), however these works suggest that coalition-centred voters are more likely to cast a vote only on the majoritarian tier rather than split their vote. By controlling for centre-left and centre-right voters and their territorial distribution, the stronghold variable in our models should control for these coalition-identity effects.

8. Please note that the observations from Marche 2010 are not included in the regression models given that there voters can no longer split their vote.

Figure 6.1: Coalition vote gaps and party split-ticket voting by coalition, pooled data (1995-2010)

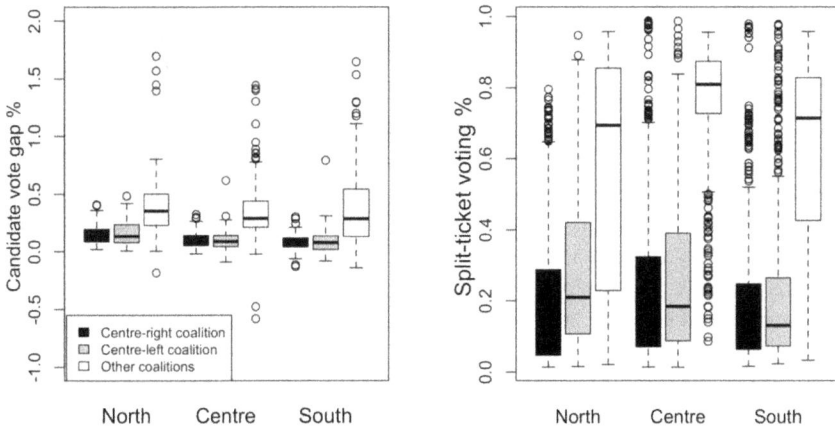

Notes: The vote gap is calculated as the percentage vote difference between the votes gained by the coalition/candidate and the parties endorsing that coalition/candidate at the provincial district level. Values of split-ticket voting has been obtained using the Rosen *et al.* (2001) method and they represent percentages of party-level split-ticket voting at the provincial district level.

Source: own elaboration from data available at www.elezionistorico.interno.it. (accessed July 2015.)

difference between the two big coalitions (centre-left and centre-right) and the smaller ones where the latter tend to obtain larger vote gaps. On the right, Figure 6.1 shows percentages of split voting by party (on the total of the party vote) at the provincial district level as estimated by the Rosen *et al.* (2001) method. The figure indicates that values of split-ticket voting are much higher for smaller coalitions when compared to the two big coalitions, which usually obtain values of split-ticket voting below 30 per cent. With regard to macro areas of the country, the vote gaps seem slightly lower in the centre and the south of the country while split-ticket voting does not appear to be higher in a specific area of the country over another. Only the centre-left coalition tends to be negatively affected by ticket-splitting in the north of the country. Generally speaking, the results indicate that the smaller the size of the party, the higher the defection on the plurality tier. On average voters in the north tend to remain loyal to their candidates (less split-ticket voting) more often than voters in the central regions and slightly more than voters in the southern regions.

Table 6.1 shows results for six multivariate models. In the vote gap analysis (Models 1-3) the dependent variable is the coalition vote gap. The total number of observations for each year of election is obtained by multiplying the number of coalitions contesting each provincial district by the total number of provincial districts. Models 1-3 for the vote gap are estimated using Ordinary Least Squares (OLS). As the spread of the residuals is somewhat wider toward the middle right of the graph than at the left, suggesting some heteroscedasticity, a robust option for estimating the standard errors using the Huber-White sandwich estimators is included. In addition, our dataset contains data on coalitions from 89 districts in 15 regions, so it is very possible that the scores within each district may not be independent, and this could lead to residuals that are not independent within districts. Consequently I treat errors as clustered by district within regions. When it comes to split-ticket voting, the dependent variable measures the percentage of split voting by party on the total of the party vote at the provincial district level as estimated by the Rosen *et al.* (2001) method. Because in this case the dependent variable is constituted by estimates, I employ Weighted Least Squares (WLS) regression as discussed in Chapter Three of this book. Models 4-6 are estimated using, again, robust errors with provincial district being clustered in regions. Finally, because the models in Table 6.1 employ pooled data (1995-2010), four dummy variable, one for each year of election, are included in the models (but not shown in the table).

Table 6.1: Explaining coalition-level vote gap and party-level split-ticket voting, pooled data (1995–2010)

	Dependent variable: COALITION vote gap (OLS)			Dependent variable: PARTY split-ticket vote (WLS)		
	(Model 1)	(Model 2)	(Model 3)	(Model 4)	(Model 5)	(Model 6)
Incumbent candidate	–0.03***		–0.04**	–0.05**		–0.01
	(0.01)		(0.01)	(0.02)		(0.02)
Party leader candidate	0.08***		0.09***	–0.09***		–0.09***
	(0.01)		(0.01)	(0.03)		(0.02)
1st place	–0.26***		–0.24***	–0.60***		–0.60***
	(0.01)		(0.02)	(0.02)		(0.03)
2nd place	–0.24***		–0.21***	–0.51***		–0.56***
	(0.01)		(0.01)	(0.04)		(0.03)
1st X district competitiveness	0.02		0.02	–0.22*		–0.04
	(0.05)		(0.05)	(0.09)		(0.09)
2nd X district competitiveness	–0.01		–0.01	–0.33*		–0.25*
	(0.05)		(0.04)	(0.13)		(0.11)
Lower X district competitiveness	0.13		0.12	–0.01		0.03
	(0.14)		(0.14)	(0.09)		(0.08)
Policy-congruent coalition		–0.14***	–0.00		–0.29***	–0.04*
		(0.01)	(0.01)		(0.03)	(0.02)
Coalition experience		–0.15***	–0.05**		–0.32***	–0.02
		(0.02)	(0.01)		(0.03)	(0.02)

(Continued)

Table 6.1: Explaining coalition-level vote gap and party-level split-ticket voting, pooled data (1995–2010) (Continued)

	Dependent variable: COALITION vote gap (OLS)			Dependent variable: PARTY split-ticket vote (WLS)		
	(Model 1)	(Model 2)	(Model 3)	(Model 4)	(Model 5)	(Model 6)
Frustrated party					−0.09***	0.06***
					(0.02)	(0.01)
Small party					0.21***	0.14***
					(0.03)	(0.02)
Party stronghold			0.03			−0.06**
			(0.02)			(0.02)
Number of SMD	0.01*	0.02***	0.01*	0.02*	0.06***	0.03**
candidates	(0.00)	(0.01)	(0.00)	(0.01)	(0.01)	(0.01)
PR Threshold	−0.05	−0.09	−0.05	0.01	0.13***	0.01
	(0.03)	(0.08)	(0.03)	(0.03)	(0.03)	(0.01)
Constant	0.29***	0.23***	0.29***	0.56***	0.11	0.54***
	(0.03)	(0.02)	(0.03)	(0.06)	(0.08)	(0.06)
Observations	1412	1412	1412	4149	4149	4149
Adjusted R^2	0.304	0.231	0.308	0.615	0.453	0.658
AIC	−603.35	−466.35	−608.39	−467.06	987.35	−948.77

Notes: Robust standard errors in parentheses: *$p < 0.05$, **$p < 0.01$, ***$p < 0.001$.

Model 1 for the vote gap and Model 4 for the split-ticket voting respectively show the effect of candidate-specific factors. An incumbent candidate has the effect of decreasing both the vote gap and split-ticket voting, whereas running a party leader increases the vote gap and it reduces the amount of split-ticket voting. As introduced previously, if anything, one expects the competitiveness of the district race in Italy to have a positive effect for the vote gap and a negative effect for split-ticket voting in the case of the two-top ranked candidates. These results would be in-line with personal voting for candidates rather than strategic considerations. Table 6.1 demonstrates that this is indeed what I find but only for split-ticket voting, whereas all the district variables are insignificant in the vote gap model.

Model 2 for the vote gap and Model 5 for the split-ticket voting show the effect of pre-electoral coalition-specific factors. Running a policy-congruent coalition and coalition experience are both likely to decrease the vote gap and they reduce defection as expected. Because the analysis of split-ticket voting is at the party level, Model 5 includes controls for the size of the party entering the coalition as well as whether or not the party runs its own candidate. The results in Table 6.1 suggest that junior coalition partners are characterised by higher percentages of split-ticket vote than large coalition partners. Similarly parties that do not present their own candidate are characterised by higher levels of split-ticket voting. Running complete models (Models 3 and 6) increases the explanatory power as the higher value of the Adjusted R-squared suggests. In complete models the size and the effect of candidate-specific variables remain about the same, whereas coalition- and district-specific factors have a much lower effect. Table 1 also shows that long-term socio-political voting predictors are important to explain loyalty to the coalition: where parties are historically strong I find higher vote gaps and lower levels of split-ticket voting despite only for the latter the results are statistically significant.

In summary, the two models, vote gap and split-ticket voting, show different results. The multivariate findings suggest that pre-electoral coalition features are important to explain both the vote gap and split-ticket voting: they represent the gluing effect which helps parties retaining its voters on the majoritarian tier. On the other hand, the features of the candidate relate more to the magnetic effect, which helps to explain whether or not the candidate is able to attract votes beyond the traditional base of the parties linked to it. Above all, the variables associated with the voter's party (e.g., whether the party is small; whether the party is ideologically close to the other parties in the pre-electoral coalition; whether the candidate on the majoritarian ballot is from his own party) affect the pattern of vote gap and split-ticket voting, suggesting that voters are paying primary attention to party factors in deciding how to vote. In contrast, I find no evidence the district-specific factors affect voting, suggesting very low levels of strategic voting.

The results for the threshold variable indicate a negative effect on the vote gap but a slightly positive and significant effect on split-ticket voting. The expectation originally developed was that, if anything, a higher electoral threshold should have decreased the level of ticket-splitting to keep intact the chances of a party to get seats after the elections. So despite the fact that the results are only marginally significant and the impact very low, the findings run against the original expectation. This, however, may simply be an artefact due to the fact that among the three regions that have increased the electoral threshold, two of them, i.e. Calabria and Toscana, are usually characterised by the highest level of split-ticket voting. For this reason, even if it is true that a higher electoral threshold has decreased vote switching in these regions, this change is not being appreciated by the statistical models. Checking for the effects of other modifications of the electoral rules in a similar manner again shows no consistent effects on vote choice. I expect, however, that in future elections, with more regions adopting modifications and voters and parties learning and adjusting their behaviour, these reforms can impact electoral behaviour in interesting ways.

Finally with regard to number of candidates/coalitions contesting the SMD tier, one expects that the presence of a larger number of candidates will decrease vote gaps and increase split ticket voting; the results in Table 6.1 indicate that the variable controlling for the number of candidates running in each district, has significant positive effects on both the vote gaps and split-ticket voting, indicating that the features of the electoral competition have an independent effect on vote choice beyond voters' preferences.

An extension of the aggregate-level analysis is carried out in Appendix 6.II using surveys. In this case, the dependent variable is dichotomous, whether or not the voter casts a split-ticket vote. The findings are broadly consistent across surveys and aggregate data. First and foremost the effect of candidate features, such as incumbency, is again negative but it is very small and fails to show significance across all models. With regard to district competitiveness, I again find results in line with personal voting for candidates rather than strategic considerations. Concerning coalition-specific effects, I can confirm that a policy-congruent coalition is likely to reduce defection. However, the variable coalition experience is now not statistically significant. The findings also suggest that voters with higher levels of political interest are less likely to split as one would have expected from the analysis of the electoral system rules. The model also tells us that having a party attachment decreases the probability of splitting the ticket.

Summary

Scholars of voting behaviour under mixed-member electoral systems have often highlighted that split-ticket voting is a result of strategic behaviour. Previous findings in this book have shown that the framework strategic/sincere voting is not always an appropriate one to account for the variation observed. In particular, the comparative analysis explained that the two votes tend to be very similar when it comes to influence of sincere and strategic voting predictors. Notwithstanding, it was clear that the PR vote is much more party-centred than the SMD, which remains better explained by candidates' features and preferences. The Japanese case study, through the use of both aggregate and survey data, has confirmed the intuition from the comparative chapter showing that strategic voting is a residual category of split-ticket voting and that the two votes are cast differently by voters.

The main focus of the analysis conducted in this chapter has been on the effect of intentions versus formal electoral rules and party supply on split-ticket voting. The peculiarity of the Italian mixed system has indeed permitted to shed light on the effects of long-term voting attitudes when compared to the influence of short-term factors such as parties and candidates appeal. Furthermore, the peculiar Italian mixed system where pre-electoral coalitions are displayed on the electoral ballot permitted an additional investigation on the forced nature of split-ticket voting resulting from elite coordination on the SMD aimed at preventing voters from splitting to other coalitions. The analysis of forced voters suggests that the features of the district race are important determinants of party defection and they have a significant effect on both the vote gaps and split-ticket voting. Notwithstanding, the analysis confirms that voter preferences remain paramount to explain the observed variation. The fact that the forced variable explains relatively less than one would have expected indicates that forced voters would have probably split their ticket anyway. This confirms the findings in the Japanese setting where I found that it is not the nature of force that matters to predict split-ticket voting but rather whether or not voters pick candidates and then parties or vice versa. Moreover, the relationship between strategic vote and split-ticket voting is more complicated than the current literature would suggest and most of what appears consistent with a strategic hypothesis, at a closer look, reveals to be in line with personal voting and/or the results of the limited choice voters have on the majoritarian ballot here in terms of pre-electoral coalitions.

With regard to socio-political features, the analysis in the Italian case shows that intentional and unintentional sources of split-ticket voting are mediated by the social and cultural context in which people cast their vote. Intentions concern sincere and strategic voting whereas unintentional sources refer to the electoral rules and the features of the district race. Voters from some areas will be more or less likely to split than others in different areas of the same country regardless of what is on offer on the electoral ballot. Ultimately, the Italian case showed that long-term features of the electorate have a rather important effect and consequently, the literature on split-ticket voting should take them into account when examining vote choice.

PART III

THEORETICAL IMPLICATIONS

Chapter Seven

Conclusion and Directions for Future Research

Summary

At the heart of this book is the narrow question: why, in mixed-member electoral systems, do citizens split their vote by choosing a party and then a candidate affiliated with a different party? The book shows that the answer to this question is more nuanced than one might expect. Furthermore, the manner in which voters split their ticket has far-reaching implications on a wide range of theoretical explanations of voting behaviour, including personalisation of politics, voters' ability to strategically work within the institutions of representative democracy, as well as on the effect of institutions and political rules on how people vote. The present study differs from previous research in several ways.

To start with, the literature on vote choice under mixed rules relies on a general assumption that party preference is the yardstick for both the party and the candidate vote (Pappi and Thurner 2002: 215). A first point of departure from the current literature this book takes is to relax the assumption that vote choice is party-centred. In fact, the party vote is an endogenous product of an election in which the voter is also being asked to vote for a candidate, and we should recognise that some voters may start by choosing a majoritarian candidate and follow the candidate to a party with her proportional vote. Given the changes in many party systems over the past twenty years (e.g., Dalton 2000), one has to acknowledge the existence of many non-aligned or loosely-aligned voters, whose party vote choice is influenced by who is running on the majoritarian tier, especially so in countries such as Japan. To free the analysis from the party-centred assumption several steps have been taken in this book. In the first step, the measurement of the dependent variable has been altered: the two votes, the party and the candidate vote, have been analysed separately rather than in conjunction as commonly done. Thus, in this book, the dependent variable is not split-ticket voting, as such, but vote choice examined separately in the two parts of the ballot paper that is then analysed using the same set of covariates. The central aim is to assess whether or not there are substantial differences between the two votes when it comes to the influence of sincere, strategic and institutional factors.

There is clear evidence in this regard that the two votes are indeed different with party considerations weighting more on the proportional tier when compared to the majoritarian tier of the ballot paper where voters are asked to vote for candidates instead of parties. Some support is found for the standard argument that a vote under proportional rules is more sincere than a vote under majoritarian rules. Despite this, however, the evidence indicates that the two votes cannot be explained by using a simple strategic versus sincere voting explanation. And, as shown in the comparative analysis carried out in Chapter Four, this is equally true in a party-centred, old democracy such as Germany as it is in a candidate-centred, younger democracy, such as Japan.

Another step to free the analysis from the party-centred assumption is to analyse split-ticket voting using classical logistic models where the dependent variable is a dummy measuring the probability of splitting the ticket. However, this time the investigation has been carried out altering the measurement of the independent variables. Instead of building the independent variables as is usually done in the existing literature by considering the party vote as it comes first, all variables are measured also on the basis of the candidate voted for. For instance, the standard practice of measuring party identification variable as 1 if the respondent identifies with the party voted for on the proportional tier and 0 otherwise; in this book this classical measure is compared to a candidate-centred measure, whereby the party identification variable takes a value of 1 if the respondent identifies with the party of the candidate supported on the majoritarian tier and 0 otherwise. The comparison of the two models allows us to check whether or not voters consider the two votes similarly and to examine the extent to which the commonly used specification differs from an alternative specification of the independent variables.

I find that measuring split-ticket voting using either parties or candidates as a starting point in the analysis has an effect on substantive conclusions and, therefore, the findings from the existing literature on this subject likely provide only a limited view of the phenomenon. For one, it is clear that both party and candidate features are important determinants of split-ticket voting. The addition of candidate-centred variables reduces the effect of parties and it diminishes substantially the effect of strategic considerations on vote choice. Finally, it is clear that the two votes, the proportional and the majoritarian, are cast somewhat differently by voters whereby in the latter vote candidate features matter the most.

Another important shortcoming of the existing literature regards its exclusive focus on voter (party) preferences assuming that these are all available on the ballot paper. We know, however, that the majoritarian ballot offers always a more limited vote choice than the proportional ballot as the very small parties do not run their own candidates. Given the difficulty of studying forced vote by relying on the standard dependent variable measuring the probability of splitting the ticket, many current analyses focus primarily on non-forced voters and/or disregard the issue. One of the key aims of the book, explored in detail in Chapter Five, is to investigate whether or not forced voters behave differently from non-forced voters. In this regard, the findings indicate that it is not the type of vote – forced or non-forced – that matters to predict split-ticket voting but rather whether or not voters pick candidates and then parties or vice versa. In other words, what predicts split-ticket voting is whether the voters are party-centred or candidate-centred. Yet again, controlling for forced vote-choice reduces the power of strategic covariates and reveals that often, when not forced by the unavailability of the candidate on the majoritarian ballot, the split depends on two sincere preferences: one for a party and one for a candidate who just happens to run for another party. Ultimately, strategic voting appears to be a residual category often very difficult to disentangle from sincere voting.

The peculiarity of the Italian case in Chapter Six permits us to explore an additional aspect of forced split-ticket voting given that in this unique case pre-electoral coalitions are displayed on the electoral ballot. This final case study shows clearly that voters are paying primary attention to party factors in deciding how to vote in pre-electoral coalition-structured elections. This finding has the potential to contribute to the debate that started when Duverger (1963) explained why party systems operating under single-member district plurality electoral rules tend toward two-party competition. Duverger identified two distinct logics: voters who were trying to avoid wasting votes and wanted to make sure the less-bad candidate among the leading contestants won; and elite-level coordination aimed at conserving resources to expend on candidates who can actually win. The findings in this study suggest that elite-level coordination is doing all of the work in the majoritarian tier of mixed systems thus anticipating strategic coordination by voters.

Split-ticket voting: final reflections

At the outset of this project, I highlighted four potential contributions that this study would generate. It is now time to revisit these statements.

First, I focused on what voters are concerned with when casting a vote and the tension between preferences and motivations to influence the election outcomes. The study of strategic voting is based on the broad idea that voters are concerned with the impact of their vote on the electoral outcome. It focuses on party preferences and defines as strategic a vote that contradicts pure party-centred reasoning. As discussed in previous sections, in mixed systems this assumption is particularly problematic. Following this reasoning, the findings from this project do not negate voters' ability to act strategically. Rather, the usual picture of voters simply voting for parties is augmented by other considerations such as preferences for candidates as well as candidate availability on the ballot paper. The project clearly shows that an explanation of strategic voting has to go beyond the consideration of party preferences and incorporate the separate preferences that voters may have for parties and candidates. At the same time, it is important to account for the actual presence of certain candidates on the ballot paper. And increasingly so in future, given the widespread practice of parties across all mixed systems to coordinate, on the majoritarian ballot, thus limiting candidate choice even further.

The logic put forth in this study reinterprets the debate between the standard account of strategic and personal vote to identify the conditions under which they are likely to emerge. The analysis clearly shows that split-ticket and strategic voting on the one hand and straight and sincere voting on the other are different (empirically). The evidence suggests that split-ticket voting may be to some extent sincere and not necessarily strategic. Strategic voters, on the other hand, will act upon strategic incentives on both ballots and the vote under majoritarian rules is only slightly more likely to be impinged by strategic reasoning. This is in line with very recent findings highlighting the presence of strategic voting also under proportional rules (e.g., Blais *et al.* 2006; Bowler *et al.* 2010), I find here compatible with both threshold insurance and wasted vote considerations holding on the PR.

Second, unlike many studies of voting behaviour, this study, while focusing on individuals, examines the logic voters employ as one that is embedded in, affected by, and reflecting particular political contexts. By doing so, this project integrates institutional contexts into the analysis of voter choice. The cross-country analysis demonstrates that different institutional environments may lead voters to make different decisions with regard to party and/or candidate strategic votes. I find interesting differences across types of mixed systems and level of experience with electoral rules. Proportional mixed systems such as Germany differ from mixed-majoritarian ones like Italy and Japan in that they provide less evidence of personal voting. This can be a consequence of party strategies and their coordination efforts on the candidate ballot in majoritarian mixed systems such as Japan and Italy. When it comes to the group of newer democracies, the patterns of vote choice are quite heterogeneous across countries but overall it seems that parties impinge on both voters less overall than in more established democracies. Ultimately, this means that the simple presence of strategic incentives does not mean that voters will necessarily act upon them.

Third, this project speaks to the literature on vote choice from a methodological point of view. Electoral behaviour research is not unique in that researchers often need to use aggregate data to infer individual-level relationships. This is either because surveys are not available or because the main interest lies in the geographical variation of specific patterns and surveys do not usually provide enough data to appreciate this variation (see also Gschwend *et al.* 2003). It is well known, however, that the ecological fallacy problem is encountered when outcomes are measured at an aggregate level since the relationship between the group-level variables may be different from the relationship between variables measured at the individual level. Because aggregate data are readily available and can help researchers answer a multitude of theoretically interesting questions, the need arises to ascertain the accuracy and efficacy of the available methods to estimate disaggregated values starting from aggregate data.

The analysis conducted in Chapter Three shows that the available estimations techniques perform remarkably well over time and across settings. In particular, since the point estimates are close enough to the actual values, when used in regression models, they provide similar results to the ones obtained using the actual values. Additionally, the present results strongly encourage researchers to make use of aggregate data and aggregate estimation techniques because these have been shown to work. Criticism and limitations should not serve as an excuse to use older methods such as the limited measure of the candidate vote gap. Beyond that, the project shows that it is ultimately the combination of individual and aggregate-level data, i.e. surveys and election results that enables us to study vote choice in a more comprehensive and more nuanced manner.

Last, as a final reflection on vote choice, I discuss below how well the explanations focused on split-ticket voting can be applied to other contexts and how they relate to our knowledge of voting behaviour more generally.

General theoretical implications

Broadly speaking, the analysis conducted in this book illustrates that many voters like more than one party equally or prefer the most a candidate not affiliated with the most preferred party and will weight these preferences on the two tiers of the ballot paper. Voters with strong party attachment are more likely to use the party shortcut by casting a straight vote because for them parties weighs the most on both tiers of the ballot paper. When the split is not sincere and it is not forced by the unavailability of the preferred candidate, it is an attempt to maximise the impact of the two votes on the electoral outcome. The strategic ticket-splitting notwithstanding, across countries in this investigation only (much) less than 10 per cent of the voters are truly strategic. The broader picture that emerges is the one of a 'simple' voter with 'sophisticated' preferences. Parties still function as the principal cue for voting, but voters appear sophisticated in that they often like more than one party. The two-vote system allows voters to express a more nuanced electoral choice and from the analysis conducted in this book, mixed-member electoral systems appear to be the 'best of both worlds' (Shugart and Wattenberg 2003) for voters; at least for those who have sophisticated preferences.

Another important finding regards the rationale of the voting act. Despite mixed systems having arguably some of the most complicated electoral rules of all, there is no evidence supporting the conclusion that ticket-splitting is a consequence of voters' confusion with the electoral rules. Highly educated and sophisticated voters are likely to respond to strategic incentives and the district-level features play a significant role in this regard. In some cases patterns of voting appear to reflect the findings from recent studies in proportional systems stressing that voters do consider the impact of their vote on policy when casting their vote (e.g. Blais *et al.* 2006; Meffert and Gschwend 2010). This is ultimately significant for our understanding of the process of electoral democracy and should discourage claims about voters not being able to cope with the electoral rules.

A final important implication of the present book is of a methodological nature. It clearly emerges that substantive results are often, if not always, a consequence of the data at our disposal and this is particularly significant in cases where the object of interest, in this case split-ticket voting, is difficult to gauge with commonly available data. In fact, deeper investigations of split-ticket voting using both extensive individual-level survey data as well as aggregate electoral results reveal that most of what is consistent with strategic behaviour at the aggregate level is instead a result of either sincere misaligned preferences for parties and candidates or a consequence of a limited vote choice menu. The misleading conclusions are due to the lack of proper information, which have forced scholars to rely on assumptions regarding party preferences that, when tested, do not hold true. This ultimately means that whenever possible, scholars should use more than one type of data to validate their results. This dusts-off an old issue in the US and elsewhere as discussed in Chapter One: interpreting vote choice from observed behaviours is deeply problematic. This book shows clearly that split-ticket and strategic voting on the one hand and straight and sincere voting on the other are conceptually and empirically distinct.

Levels of split-ticket voting are expected to rise in the long run. This will be a consequence of parties' strategic coordination, which will restrict vote choice even further on the majoritarian ballot. Higher levels of ticket-splitting are also expected as a consequence of the fact that candidates are increasingly judged by voters independently of the parties they represent. This reflects patterns in contemporary politics characterised by an increased attention to the political protagonists, such as individual candidates and leaders instead of political issues (Caprara *et al.* 2006; Schoen and Schumann 2007) as well as a decline in party identification (e.g., Dalton 2000). Furthermore, as voters become increasingly familiar with the electoral rules and thus more likely to act strategically, they may become more inclined to engage in complex patterns of voting behaviour, including split-ticket voting. In any case, vote switching becomes a crucial area to explore to understand voters and their choices, and to appreciate the workings of elections and democracy generally. These investigations should be made easier by the increasing availability of data at both the individual and aggregate levels in older and newer democracies.

Directions for future research

The work conducted in this book raises some intriguing issues, which merit further investigation beyond countries using mixed-member electoral systems. To start with, the book has shown that vote choice cannot be explained in terms of a simple strategic versus sincere voting dichotomy. In more general terms, this book suggests the need to abandon the 'strategic versus sincere' party-centred framework as the latter seems inadequate for capturing the complexity of vote choice patterns. Looking at sophisticated voters, defined as those who favour more than one party or consider candidates irrespective of their party's affiliation, might open up new avenues of research including, but not limited to, the study of protest voting.

Moreover, it appears that voters think ahead about what is likely to happen after the elections in terms of coalition bargaining before and after the elections. In terms of post-electoral coalition building, a future line of investigation may build on this conclusion taking into account whether or not, and how, these sophisticated preferences correlate with patterns of voting behaviour beyond mixed systems. Only recently scholars have turned their attention to examining empirically whether voters consider the impact of their vote on policy (e.g., Hobolt and Karp 2010). The proposed line of investigation will consider to what extent voters are party-centred and/or candidate-centred compared to coalition-centred while taking into account policymaking institutions in each country. As this investigation can be potentially conducted in every country, yet outside a few countries little prior work exists, this naturally opens up avenues for further research in a multitude of electoral settings.

Not least the analysis can be expanded by looking into the effect of pre-electoral agreements on vote choice, a subject of political science that cries out for research. Indicative of this lack of research is the claim by Gschwend and Hooghe (2008: 557) that: 'At present, there is no research available on the question of how voters respond to the formation of pre-electoral coalitions'. This has important implications for party strategies as demonstrated in Chapter Six: while parties are still the decisive actors in the government formation process, they are restricted in their choices by the coalition preferences of the electorate, which they need to take into account.

This book has also shown that the nature of the vote choice (such as the number of parties and candidates running for elections, competitiveness of the district race and so forth) matters more when individuals vote for candidates rather than for parties; however, national issues have a larger impact on the party vote. These findings hold true across countries as diverse as Japan, Germany, New Zealand and Italy. This conclusion raises some interesting questions about the link between voters and elected officials when voters are asked to vote for candidates as opposed to when they are asked to vote for parties. This can potentially provide the basis for a future line of investigation, which looks at the degree of congruence between voters and elected officials and how different this congruence is when people vote directly for parties rather than for candidates. Despite the importance of 'congruence' between voters and parties for representative democracy (Adams and Ezrow 2009; Powell 2009; Golder and Stramski 2010), little is known today about whether the link between voters and elected officials is different across countries adopting different electoral rules. To conduct this analysis, one needs first to define a theoretical model that establishes the dimensionality of the political space as well as the link between voters, parties and candidates. Thus, such a developed theoretical framework can be tested and applied to several countries to conduct case studies and large-n analyses.

To conclude, this book contributes to theories of vote choice and party competition. By challenging common theoretical assumptions and existing empirical methods within the study of vote choice under mixed-member electoral systems, the present study contributes to an ongoing debate about citizens' preferences and motivations as well as the extent to which parties and candidates shape voting behaviour and influence the working of electoral democracy.

APPENDICES

Deterministic and statistical approaches to ecological inference

Two long-standing methods proposed to tackle the ecological fallacy issue are the 'Methods of Bounds' (Duncan and Davis 1953) and the 'Ecological Regression' (Goodman 1953, 1959) (hereafter referred to as Goodman's method). The former produces bounds that must be correct without relying on any statistical assumption. The intuition behind these quantities is that if T_A^i is 36 and X_A^i is 70 then β_{AA}^i must lie between 0 and 36. Therefore, the Methods of Bounds only returns an interval and no point estimate is produced - how informative the deterministic bounds are depends on the nature of the data. Estimates of the quantities of interest are instead provided by Goodman's method. Goodman formalises the logic of the approach in a simple regression model where the relationship to be studied is a linear one. Let X^i be the proportion of the population in area i that belongs to group 1, $1\text{-}X^i$ the proportion of the population in area i that belongs to group 2, and Y^i the proportion of the population in area i with the characteristics or choice at issue. Goodman demonstrates that the accounting identity $Y^i = \beta^{1i} X^i + \beta^{2i}(1\text{–}X^i)$ holds exactly (see De Sio (2003) for an explanation of how the identity expands to larger tables). The key assumption necessary for unbiasedness is that the parameters and X^i are uncorrelated. Where this assumption does not hold the estimates will be biased, and even outside the deterministic bounds (King *et al.* 2004). Several have shown as the assumption of unbiasedness is often violated in the context of electoral studies (e.g., Achen and Shively 1995; Cleave *et al.* 1995; King 1997; Tam Cho and Gaines 2004). The assumption of constant parameters is relaxed in some subsequent models such as the Neighborhood (Freedman *et al.* 1991) and Thomsen's (1987) models (for an early review of these methods see Cleave *et al.* [1995]; for a recent discussion see Park *et al.* [2014]).

King's (1997) revolutionary idea was to combine the information from the bounds, applied to quantities of interest for each and every ecological unit, with a statistical approach for extracting information within the bounds (Achen and Shively 1995; Liu 2007). In a nutshell, the estimation procedure is as follows. First, it is hypothesised that the parameters follow a truncated bivariate normal distribution. The parameters of this distribution are obtained by maximum likelihood estimation, carried out through Monte Carlo simulations. Second, it is assumed that the data do not exhibit any spatial autocorrelation. Last, the parameters are assumed to be uncorrelated with the regressors; in other words, no 'aggregation bias' is present (King 1997: 55). There is an ongoing debate about the merits of King's method. The most critical scrutiny of this method comes from scholars who have questioned the model's assumptions and the consequences of these assumptions being violated (Tam Cho and Gaines 2004; Cho 1998).

King's (1997) method has been surpassed by a more complex one suggested by King et al. (1999): it is a hierarchical Bayesian model using Markov chain Monte Carlo (MCMC) technology (Tanner 1996) based on the combination of two specific models, one assuming a bimodal distribution for the variance between ecological units and one based on a beta distribution for the within unit variance. A key advantage of this method is that it generalises immediately to arbitrarily large RxC tables. (The extension of the hierarchical models to the RxC case has been considered for instance by Brown and Payne (1986) as discussed by Wakefield (2004: 417)). The extensions to a large RxC table is very important in the context of the study of split-ticket voting. Indeed, the seminal method suggested by King (1997) is designed for binary data where data are arrayed to create 2x2 contingency tables. Of course, the vote choice under mixed rules usually represents a much more complex situation given that there will almost always be more than two parties and two candidates contesting elections.

King provides a workaround, which allows his method to be used on these more complex situations via an iterative technique wherein the binary model is consecutively applied to subsets of the larger table until all cells of the table can be either estimated or calculated from the values of other cells. Ferree (2004), however, shows that combining rows or columns to produce residual or aggregate categories can cause violations of the model assumptions, even when these problems are not present in the original data. The best solution is to use methods that enable to estimate separately all rows and columns simultaneously. The tests in Chapter Three of this book focus exclusively on two methods: the Rosen et al. (2001) and the Greiner and Quinn (2009), able to perform the complex task of estimating all cells of RxC contingency tables simultaneously.

Additional remarks on estimation methods

A *desideratum* for an RxC technique is the possibility of allowing a variety of extensions. The ease with which the Rosen *et al.* (2001) and the Greiner and Quinn (2009) method may theoretically be extended is one of their appealing attributes. I consider below two of these extensions:

1. the inclusion of covariates in the estimation of the quantities of interest and
2. the use of priors in the model specification.

Please note that these issues are discussed only in relation to the study of split-ticket voting.

Covariates

Both the Rosen *et al.* (2001) and the Greiner and Quinn (2009) methods enable conditioning values of interest on a covariate. As discussed by King (1997) conditioning the parameters to vary as functions of measured covariates, allows us to 'control' for patterns of systematic variation at the unit of observation, which, in turn, helps to relax the assumption of no aggregation bias in the data, a critical assumption for any ecological inference model (see also Voss 2004). Aggregation bias may also occur when parameters values in specific unit of observations (polling station in our case) differ from the general pattern aggregated to the upper level (district level in our case). For the two methods used in Chapter Three, the addition of covariates is essentially straightforward with just a small variation in the code launched in R (how this is done for the Rosen *et al.* (2001) method see Wittenberg *et al.* (2007) or the technical report for the *eiPack* package; for the Greiner and Quinn (2009) method see Greiner *et al.* [2013]).

However, while the models are flexible enough to allow the use of covariates; the choice and the use of covariates is by no mean an easy choice. First and foremost, the analyst must consider whether the addition of covariates is appropriate in the specific context under scrutiny. The loss of information due to the aggregation is known to be large and adding complications to the basic method might demand too much from the data. When the models are applied at the polling station level, as it is the case in this book, researchers need to find covariates supposedly correlated with values of straight- and split-ticket voting that vary at the polling station level which is undoubtedly a challenging task. It is, however, easier to find district-level covariates.

Specifically, the literature on split-ticket voting argues that quantities of straight-ticket voting are somewhat negatively correlated with the competitiveness of the electoral race, where more competitive districts on average feature lower levels of straight-ticket voting. Furthermore, levels of straight-ticket voting depend on the local strength of the party as well as on the total number of candidates contesting the district race (Karp *et al.* 2002; Johnston and Pattie 2002; Benoit *et al.* 2004). I re-estimated values of interest at the district-level directly with and without covariates. As covariates I used a dummy variable controlling for specific party strongholds, a variable measuring the total number of candidates at the district level or a measure of the competitiveness of the single-member district race measured as the difference between the first and the second-best placed candidate. The results using covariates were not significantly different from those obtained without them. Similarly, Burden (2009) finds that estimates of split-ticket voting in Japan were not sensitive to the choice of the covariates.

It has to be noted, however, that the addition of covariates exponentially increases the computation time needed to reach convergence and quite often it was not possible to obtain stable results (in a reasonable amount of time). Even when collapsing columns and rows to obtain contingency tables smaller than 5X5, the two methods rarely provide results in a reasonable amount of time, that is to say within 48 hours for each district.[1] The issue was particularly severe for the EI-ML model. This might be due to the fact that covariates are not important in the settings under scrutiny in this work. Nonetheless, this should serve as a caveat for future research. Ultimately, the suggestion is to estimate quantities of interest with and without covariates for (very) small subsamples of data and only proceed with further estimations when the test of covariates suggests that these are significant (see Herron and Shotts 2003 in this regard).

Prior specification

One important part of the model specification in the context of ecological inference models is the prior specification. Indeed researchers have realised for some time that the quality of ecological inference depends critically on the quality of the prior assumptions one makes. Seemingly innocuous differences to the prior distribution assumed for the model parameters can have large effects on the resulting posterior distribution and thus on inference. Overall the choice of the priors is highly contingent on investigator assumptions (Wakefield 2004). Where observed or true behaviour of one group of interest is known and these observations are temporally (Quinn 2004) or spatially (Haneuse and Wakefield 2004) related to unobserved behaviour, information can be easily incorporated. In some other cases, past

---

1. For this study, I have used powerful computers to sift through my large volumes of data thus computer power is not an issue for us. In particular, I have obtained access to high-performance clusters comprising 154 nodes, each equipped with 8 cores (AMD Opteron at 2.30GHz) and 16 GB of RAM.

behaviour may provide precise priors to be incorporated in the estimation (Corder and Wolbrecht 2004).

In the two national contexts under investigation in this book, the true quantities of split-ticket voting are available only at the district level. For one, one could assume that the distribution of the prior observed at the district-level holds at lower levels of aggregation; but it does not need to be. There is no fix for such a situation and the only way I can see to cope with this problem is to provide a full disclosure of the assumptions and explicit consideration with regard to the priors to help and communicate the uncertainty in the estimation. The suggestion is then to re-run estimations using different priors and to rely for substantive conclusions on those providing more realistic results.

When it comes to the version of the Rosen *et al.* (2001) method employed in this paper, this strategy implements a frequentist approximation of these Bayesian models. As such, it is not Bayesian by design and does not require priors or starting values to be specified. As far as the Greiner and Quinn (2009) method is concerned, the specification of the priors is relatively straightforward with a simple variation in the code launched in R. For the tests presented in Chapter Three, I have used the default priors in the in-build R package (that is a normal hyperprior distribution for the diagonal of the covariance matrix and Inverse-Wishart hyperprior for the diagonal of the matrix parameters) given that I have noticed that these provide the closest possible values to the observed ones.

Additional remarks on regression models

The estimates provided by the EI-MD and the EI-ML methods, can be used as dependent variable in regression models aim to explain patterns of split-ticket voting at both the district or party level (also referred to as second-stage regression models where in the first stage estimates are obtained and in the second stage these estimates are used as dependent variable). The dependent variable represents the estimated percentage of party-level split-ticket voting in a certain district. To recall, the methodological literature on second-stage regression models advocates the use of the WLS (Adolph *et al.* 2003). Differently, another strand of the empirical literature, after surveying several studies using proportions as dependent variable, find evidence to reject the least square regression and two-sided Tobit model and advocates the adoption of beta regression (e.g., Kieschnick and McCullough 2003; Papke and Wooldridge 1996; Cribari-Neto and Zeileis 2010). I run a similar test below using as dependent variable the values of split-ticket voting as estimated by the Rosen *et al.* (2001) and Greiner and Quinn (2009) methods discussed in Chapter Three of this book. The aim is to test whether or not the choice of the model affects substantive conclusions.

Table A3.1 shows the results using the estimated level of split-ticket voting as the dependent variable modelling the observations using several regression techniques. Model 1 and 4 in Table A3.1 shows the results using WLS, Model 2 and 5 using Tobit regression and Model 3 and 6 using Beta regression for the EI-MD and EI-ML respectively using data from the 2008 elections in New Zealand. First and foremost, WLS and the Tobit models provide identical results, confirming the findings in Kieschnick and McCullough (2003). The beta distribution model for which Table A3.1 shows marginal effects provide results quite similar to the WLS and the Tobit models. From this analysis it is straightforward to conclude that the three models provide all very similar results and the choice of the model does not appear to affect the substantive findings. Similar conclusions are reached when using data from other years of elections in New Zealand or data from Scotland. For this reason, subsequent investigations of split-ticket voting in other chapters of this book will employ the more straightforward WLS regression.

Table A3.1: Second-stage regression models: a comparison of regression techniques, New Zealand 2008

Dependent variable:	EI-MD estimates			EI-ML estimates		
	(Model 1)	(Model 2)	(Model 3)	(Model 4)	(Model 5)	(Model 6)
	WLS	Tobit	Beta	WLS	Tobit	Beta
Incumbency	-0.147***	-0.147***	-0.275***	-0.004	-0.004	-0.014
	(0.021)	(0.021)	(0.031)	(0.003)	(0.003)	(0.008)
Gender	-0.055***	-0.055***	-0.104***	0.002	0.002	0.009
	(0.016)	(0.016)	(0.030)	(0.004)	(0.004)	(0.008)
DContention	2.292***	2.292***	0.827***	0.978***	0.978***	0.741***
	(0.072)	(0.071)	(0.002)	(0.096)	(0.096)	(0.078)
Margin	0.508***	0.508***	0.349***	-0.007	-0.007	-0.005
	(0.083)	(0.083)	(0.039)	(0.007)	(0.007)	(0.011)
N	313	313	313	312	312	312
LL	197.35	14752.11	32733.15	459.87	521.17	1324.90
AIC	-384.69	-29492.23	-65454.29	-909.74	-1030.35	-2637.79

Notes: Standard errors in parentheses: *p<.05, *p<.01, *p<.001. The dependent variable is the percentage of split-ticket voting received by each party at the district level. All models have been estimated using Stata 13. For the beta regression model the table shows marginal effects when all dummy variables are set at their mode and continuous variables at their mean; in this case I have used the betafit command in Stata 13.

APPENDIX 4.1

Data sources

Table A4.1: Countries, elections and data sources (accessed July 2015)

Country	Election years (data source)
Germany	2009 (https://dbk.gesis.org/dbksearch/SDesc2.asp?ll=10&notabs=&af =&nf=&search=GLES&search2=&db=D&no=5303) 2013 (https://dbk.gesis.org/dbksearch/sdesc2.asp?no=5703&db=d)
New Zealand	1996, 1999, 2002 (http://www.nzes.org/)
Scotland	2007 (http://discover.ukdataservice.ac.uk/ Catalogue/?sn=6026&type=Data%20catalogue) 2011(https://www.strath.ac.uk/humanities/research/cers/ scottishelectionstudy2011/)
Japan	2003, 2005 (http://csrda.iss.u-tokyo.ac.jp/en/)
Italy	2001 (http://www.itanes.org/)
Albania	2005 (CSES 2 data http://www.cses.org/)
Hungary	1998, 2002 (CSES 1 and CSES 2)
Thailand	2007 (CSES 3)
South Korea	2004, 2008 (CSES 2 and CSES 3)

Correlation between Intended and Actual vote choice for selected subgroups of voters

Table A4.2: Correlation between intended and actual vote choice for selected subgroups of voters

	Germany		New Zealand			Scotland		Italy	Japan	
	2009	2013	1996	1999	2002	2007	2011	2001	2003	2005
Party identifiers										
Intended and Actual PR	0.780	0.877	0.607	0.708	0.712	0.864	0.938	0.739	0.806	0.834
Intended and Actual SMD	0.777	0.881	0.645	0.685	0.565	0.859	0.940	0.798	0.913	0.949
diff	*0.003*	*-0.004*	*-0.038*	*0.023*	*0.147*	*0.005*	*-0.002*	*-0.059*	*-0.107*	*-0.115*
Intended PR and Intended SMD	0.738	0.852	0.478	0.470	0.468	0.866	0.893	0.765	0.707	0.644
Actual PR and Actual SMD	0.685	0.862	0.463	0.497	0.465	0.809	0.892	0.915	0.661	0.649
diff	***0.053***	*-0.010*	*0.015*	*-0.027*	*0.003*	***0.057***	*0.001*	*-0.150*	*0.046*	*-0.005*
Non-party identifiers										
Intended and Actual PR	0.762	0.876	0.567	0.696	0.684	0.853	0.887	0.774	0.771	0.795
Intended and Actual SMD	0.751	0.868	0.591	0.672	0.542	0.829	0.881	0.737	0.853	0.908
diff	*0.011*	*0.008*	*-0.024*	*0.024*	***0.142***	*0.024*	*0.006*	*0.037*	*-0.082*	*-0.113*
Intended PR and Intended SMD	0.717	0.847	0.424	0.495	0.431	0.806	0.825	0.826	0.649	0.637
Actual PR and Actual SMD	0.627	0.824	0.389	0.474	0.411	0.825	0.810	0.839	0.580	0.555
diff	***0.090***	*0.023*	*0.035*	*0.021*	*0.020*	*-0.019*	*0.015*	*-0.013*	*0.069*	***0.082***
Supporters of two best performing parties at t-1										
Intended and Actual PR	0.765	0.875	0.585	0.696	0.674	0.858	0.899	0.761	0.794	0.804
Intended and Actual SMD	0.755	0.873	0.611	0.671	0.552	0.839	0.900	0.725	0.945	0.918
diff	*0.010*	*0.002*	*-0.026*	*0.025*	***0.122***	*0.019*	*-0.001*	*0.036*	*-0.151*	*-0.114*
Intended PR and Intended SMD	0.728	0.852	0.410	0.516	0.449	0.806	0.836	0.832	0.581	0.660

(Continued)

Table A4.2: Correlation between intended and actual vote choice for selected subgroups of voters (Continued)

	Germany		New Zealand			Scotland		Italy	Japan	
	2009	2013	1996	1999	2002	2007	2011	2001	2003	2005
Actual PR and Actual SMD	0.632	0.827	0.417	0.488	0.408	0.832	0.792	0.828	0.601	0.596
diff	*0.096*	*0.025*	*-0.007*	*0.028*	*0.041*	*-0.026*	*0.044*	*0.004*	*-0.020*	*0.064*
Supporters of lower-ranked performing parties at *t-1*										
Intended and Actual PR	0.766	0.875	0.635	0.699	0.693	0.863	0.899	0.712	0.798	0.795
Intended and Actual SMD	0.755	0.873	0.578	0.677	0.557	0.844	0.900	0.799	0.943	0.902
diff	*0.011*	*0.002*	*0.057*	*0.022*	*0.136*	*0.019*	*-0.001*	*-0.087*	*-0.145*	*-0.107*
Intended PR and Intended SMD	0.728	0.852	0.443	0.492	0.454	0.814	0.836	0.731	0.655	0.633
Actual PR and Actual SMD	0.632	0.827	0.406	0.483	0.421	0.836	0.792	0.891	0.588	0.573
diff	*0.096*	*0.025*	*0.037*	*0.009*	*0.033*	*-0.022*	*0.044*	*-0.160*	*0.067*	*0.060*
N	2042	3213	1377	1522	1147	834	512	1901	795	843

Specimen of the ballot paper, Veneto 2005

Figure A6.1: Specimen of the ballot paper, Veneto 2005

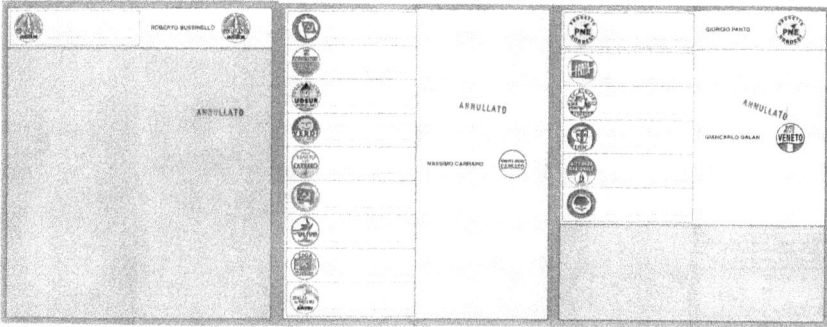

Notes: The ballot paper refers to the 2005 regional election in the region of Veneto. The ballot paper displays four coalitions. The section of the ballot paper on the left displays one coalition formed by one party, the section in the middle displays a coalition endorsed by nine parties and the section on the right displays two coalitions, one endorsed by one party and the other endorsed by five parties.

An analysis at the individual-level

This section uses surveys to extend the evidence found using aggregate data by also including individual-level determinants. It is also possible to check whether similar patterns are to be found when switching the level of observation. Even though a direct comparison between aggregate and individual level data should be done with caution (because, while the aggregate level analysis uses pooled data, surveys only cover the 2010 election) the use of individual-level data, using the same independent variables while changing the level of investigation from the party to the individual, can still provide a test for the findings presented so far. Ideally one would find that substantive results do not change when using surveys in place of aggregate data.

The dependent variable in this section is dichotomous, whether or not the voter casts a split-ticket vote. Consequently logit regression models are used with a robust option with district clustered in regions. Models 1–3 in Table 6.2 present the results using only the voting predictors used in the aggregate analysis; Model 4 uses only individual-level predictors while Model 5 presents the results obtained combining individual and aggregate-level variables. For all models presented in Table 6.2 substantive results are unchanged if a random logit is used to account for the fact that the analysis takes into account both individual and aggregate-level indicators. In addition, likelihood ratio tests suggest that the multi-level strategy is not needed.

The findings are broadly consistent both across surveys and aggregate data. First, the effect of candidate features, such as incumbency, is again negative but it is very small and fails to show significance across all models. With regard to district competitiveness the results are again remarkably similar to those obtained using aggregate data. Concerning coalition-specific effects found using aggregate data, all are confirmed with an exception made for coalition experience. The ability to predict a split-ticket vote is higher when we use coalition- or candidate-specific factors when compared to district-specific factors. Model 4 shows results including only individual-level indicators. The findings suggest that voters with higher levels of political interest are less likely to split as one would have expected from the analysis of the electoral system rules. The model also tells us that having a party attachment decreases the probability of splitting the ticket. Model 5 in Table 6.2 brings individual and aggregate-level indicators together. Whereas the broader conclusions do not change for each of the coefficients, the power of the model is now at its highest, suggesting that the simultaneous account of both factors is indeed an important one.

Table A6.1: Explaining split-ticket vote at the individual level, 2010 election: random effects logit coefficients

	Dependent variable: straight vs split-ticket voting				
	(Model 1)	(Model 2)	(Model 3)	(Model 4)	(Model 5)
Incumbent candidate	0.09		0.04		0.09
	(0.23)		(0.31)		(0.31)
Party leader	0.31		−0.19		−0.19
candidate	(0.38)		(0.39)		(0.39)
1st place	−3.47***		−3.04***		−3.08***
	(0.25)		(0.29)		(0.29)
2nd place	−2.99***		−2.80***		−2.79***
	(0.21)		(0.22)		(0.22)
1st X district	−0.42		−0.24		−0.34
competitiveness	(1.33)		(1.36)		(1.35)
2nd X district	1.47		0.22		0.13
competitiveness	(1.31)		(1.36)		(1.36)
Lower X district	5.06**		4.07*		4.33**
competitiveness	(1.63)		(1.63)		(1.64)
Policy-congruent		−1.68***	−0.89***		−0.84***
coalition		(0.28)	(0.25)		(0.25)
Coalition experience		−0.08	−0.10		−0.14
		(0.22)	(0.26)		(0.26)
Frustrated party		−0.24	−0.13		−0.16
		(0.13)	(0.16)		(0.16)
Small party		0.73***	0.72***		0.78***
		(0.19)	(0.20)		(0.20)
Party stronghold		−0.88***	−0.62**		−0.66**
		(0.19)	(0.23)		(0.23)
Number of SMD	0.19	0.14	0.20		0.20
candidates	(0.10)	(0.10)	(0.11)		(0.10)
PR Threshold	0.30	0.30	0.26		0.30
	(0.34)	(0.31)	(0.34)		(0.34)
Party identification				−0.55***	−0.66***
				(0.14)	(0.15)
Education				−0.34*	−0.46**
				(0.13)	(0.14)
Political interest				−0.42***	−0.37***
				(0.10)	(0.11)

(Continued)

Table A6.1: Explaining split-ticket vote at the individual level, 2010 election: random effects logit coefficients (Continued)

	Dependent variable: straight vs split-ticket voting				
	(Model 1)	(Model 2)	(Model 3)	(Model 4)	(Model 5)
Constant	−0.90	−2.41***	−0.67	−1.90***	−0.22
	(0.53)	(0.51)	(0.57)	(0.10)	(0.57)
Observations	5038	5038	5038	5038	5038
Groups	74	74	74	74	74
LL	−1414.02	−1530.88	−1391.86	−1561.79	−1368.51
Rho	0.21	0.20	0.20	0.04	0.21
	(0.04)	(0.06)	(0.04)	(0.01)	(0.04)

Notes: Entries are results from random-effects logit models. Standard errors in parenthesis: *$p < 0.05$, **$p < 0.01$, ***$p < 0.001$. The models include only respondents who cast both votes. Sample respondents who cast both a party and a candidate vote are as follows (with regional population as for 2013 in parenthesis): 478 respondents in Piemonte (population 4,436,798), 1,034 in Lombardia (9,973,397), 550 in Veneto (4,926,818), 163 in Liguria (1,591,939), 497 in Emilia-Romagna (4,446,354), 376 in Toscana (3,750,511), 70 in Umbria (896,742), 642 in Lazio (5,870,451), 564 in Campania (5,869,965), 366 in Puglia (4,090,266), 73 in Basilicata (578,391) and 225 in Calabria (1,980,533).

Source: Ipsos opinion poll regional elections 2010.

Bibliography

Abramowitz, A. I. (1991) 'Incumbency, campaign spending, and the decline of competition in US house elections', *The Journal of Politics*, 53(1): 34–56.

Abramson, P. R., Aldrich, J. H., Blais, A., Diamond, M., Diskin, A., Indridason, I. H., Lee, D. J. and Levine, R. (2010) 'Comparing strategic voting under FPTP and PR', *Comparative Political Studies*, 43(1): 61–90.

Achen, C. and Shively, W. (1995), *Cross-level Inference*, University of Chicago Press.

Adams, J. and Ezrow, L. (2009) 'Who do European parties represent? How Western European parties represent the policy preferences of opinion leaders', *The Journal of Politics*, 71(1): 206–223.

Adolph, C., King, G., Herron, M. and Shotts, K. (2003) 'A consensus on second-stage analyses in ecological inference models', *Political Analysis*, 11(1): 86–94.

Agnew, J. A. (2002) *Place and Politics in Modern Italy*, Chicago: University of Chicago Press.

Alesina, A. and Rosenthal, H. (1995) *Partisan Politics, Divided Government, and the Economy*, Cambridge: Cambridge University Press.

Allison, P. D. (2001) *Missing data*, Sage University Papers Series on Quantitative Applications in the Social Sciences, Series 07-136, Thousand Oaks, CA: Sage.

Alvarez, R. M. and Nagler, J. (1998) 'When politics and models collide: Estimating models of multiparty elections', *American Journal of Political Science*, 42(1): 55–96.

— (2000) 'A new approach for modelling strategic voting in multiparty elections', *British Journal of Political Science*, 30(1): 57–75.

Alvarez, R. M. and Schousen, M. M. (1993) 'Policy moderation or conflicting expectations? Testing the intentional models of split-ticket voting', *American Politics Quarterly*, 21(4): 410–438.

Ames, B., Baker, A. and Renno, L. (2009) 'Split-ticket voting as the rule: Voters and permanent divided government in Brazil', *Electoral Studies*, 28(1): 8–20.

Asano, M. and Yanai, Y. (2013) *Stata ni yoru Keiryoseijigaku [Quantitative Methods in Political Science Using Stata]*, Tokyo: Ohmsha.

Banducci, S., Karp, J. and Vowles, J. (1998) 'Vote splitting under MMP', in J. Vowles (ed.) *Voters' Victory?: New Zealand's first election under proportional representation*, Auckland University Press, pp. 101–119.

Bargsted, M. A. and Kedar, O. (2009) 'Coalition-targeted Duvergerian voting: How expectations affect voter choice under proportional representation', *American Journal of Political Science*, 53(2): 307–323.

Bawn, K. (1999) 'Voter responses to electoral complexity: ticket splitting, rational voters and representation in the Federal Republic of Germany', *British Journal of Political Science*, 29(3): 487–505.

Bean, C. S. and Wattenberg, M. P. (1998) 'Attitudes towards divided government and ticket-splitting in Australia and the United States', *Australian Journal of Political Science*, 33(1): 25–36.

Beck, P., Baum, L., Clausen, A. and Smith Jr, C. (1992) 'Patterns and sources of ticket splitting in subpresidential voting', *American Political Science Review*, 86(4): 916–928.

Bellucci, P. and Segatti, P. (2011) *Votare in Italia. Dall'appartenenza alla scelta*, Bologna: Il Mulino.

Benoit, K. (2005) 'Hungary: holding back the tiers', in M. Gallagher and P. Mitchell (eds) *The Politics of Electoral Systems*, Oxford: Oxford University Press, pp. 231–252.

Benoit, K. and Marsh, M. (2008) 'The campaign value of incumbency: a new solution to the puzzle of less effective incumbent spending', *American Journal of Political Science*, 52(4): 874–890.

Benoit, K., Giannetti, D. and Laver, M. (2006) 'Voter strategies with restricted choice menus', *British Journal of Political Science*, 36(3): 459–485.

Benoit, K., Laver, M. and Giannetti, D. (2004) 'Multiparty Split-Ticket Voting Estimation as an Ecological Inference Problem', in K. Gary, M. A. Tanner, and O. Rosen (eds) *Ecological Inference: New methodological strategies*, Cambridge: Cambridge University Press, pp. 330–350.

Bernhagen, P. and Marsh, M. (2010) 'Missing voters, missing data: using multiple imputation to estimate the effects of low turnout', *Journal of Elections, Public Opinion and Parties*, 20(4): 447–472.

Blais, A., Aldrich, J. H., Indridason, I. H. and Levine, R. (2006) 'Do voters vote for government coalitions? Testing Downs' pessimistic conclusion', *Party Politics*, 12(6): 691–705.

Blais, A., Nadeau, R., Gidengil, E. and Nevitte, N. (2001) 'Measuring strategic voting in multiparty plurality elections', *Electoral Studies*, 20(3): 343–352.

Blais, A., Young, R. and Turcotte, M. (2005) 'Direct or indirect? Assessing two approaches to the measurement of strategic voting', *Electoral Studies*, 24(2): 163–176.

Bowler, S. and Denemark, D. (1993) 'Split ticket voting in Australia: dealignment and inconsistent votes reconsidered', *Australian Journal of Political Science*, 28(1): 19–37.

Bowler, S. and Farrell, D. M. (1995) 'Voter strategies under preferential electoral systems: a single transferable vote mock ballot survey of London voters.' *British Elections & Parties Yearbook*, 5(1): 14–31.

Bowler, S., Karp, J. and Donovan, T. (2010) 'Strategic coalition voting: Evidence from New Zealand', *Electoral Studies*, 29(3): 350–357.

Brown, P. J. and Payne, C. D. (1986) 'Aggregate data, ecological regression, and voting transitions', *Journal of the American Statistical Association*, 81 (394): 452–460.

Burden, B. (2009) 'Candidate-driven ticket splitting in the 2000 Japanese elections', *Electoral Studies*, 28(1): 33–40.

Burden, B. and Helmke, G. (2009) 'The comparative study of split-ticket voting', *Electoral Studies*, 28(1): 1–7.

Burden, B. and Kimball, D. (1998) 'A new approach to the study of ticket splitting', *American Political Science Review*, 92(3): 533–544.

Burden, B. and Kimball, D. (2004) *Why Americans Split their Tickets: Campaigns, competition, and divided government*, Ann Arbor: University of Michigan Press.

Campbell, A., Gurin, G. and Miller, W. E. (1954) *The Voter Decides*, Evanston: Row, Peterson & Co.

Campbell, A. and Miller, W. (1957) 'The motivational basis of straight and split ticket voting', *The American Political Science Review*, 51(2): 293–312.

Caprara, G. V., Schwartz, S., Capanna, C., Vecchione, M. and Barbaranelli, C. (2006) 'Personality and politics: values, traits, and political choice', *Political Psychology*, 27(1): 1–28.

Carey, J. M. and Shugart, M. S. (1995) 'Incentives to cultivate a personal vote: a rank ordering of electoral formulas', *Electoral Studies*, 14(4): 417–439.

Carman, C. and Johns, R. (2010) 'Linking coalition attitudes and split-ticket voting: the Scottish Parliament elections of 2007', *Electoral Studies*, 29(3): 381–391.

Carrubba, C. and Timpone, R. J. (2005) 'Explaining vote switching across first- and second-order elections evidence from Europe', *Comparative Political Studies*, 38(3): 260–281.

Carter, E. and Farrell, D. M. (2010) 'Electoral systems and election management', in L. LeDuc, R. G. Niemi and P. Norris (eds) *Comparing Democracies 3*, London: Sage Publications, pp. 25–44.

Cartocci, R. (1990) *Elettori in Italia: riflessioni sulle vicende elettorali degli anni ottanta*, Bologna: Il Mulino.

Carty, R. K. and Eagles, M. (1999) 'Do local campaigns matter? Campaign spending, the local canvass and party support in Canada', *Electoral Studies*, 18(1): 69–87.

Chiaramonte, A. and D'Alimonte, R. (2000) *Il maggioritario regionale: le elezioni del 16 aprile 2000*, Bologna, Il Mulino.

Cho, W.K. Tam (1998) 'If the assumption fits…: A comment on the King ecological inference solution', *Political Analysis*, 7(1): 143–163.

Cleave, N., Brown, P. and Payne, C. (1995) 'Evaluation of methods for ecological inference', *Journal of the Royal Statistical Society. Series A (Statistics in Society)*, 158(1): 55–72.

Cohen, J. and Cohen, P. (1975) *Applied Multiple Regression/Correlation Analysis for the Behavioral Sciences*, Mahwah, N.J.: Lawrence Erlbaum.

Converse, P. E. and Pierce, R. (1986) (eds) *Political Representation in France*, Cambridge, MA: Belknap Press of Harvard University Press.

Corbetta, P., Parisi, A. M. L. and Schadee, H. M. A. (1988) *Elezioni in Italia. Struttura e tipologia delle consultazioni politiche*, Bologna, Il Mulino.

Corder, K. J. and Wolbrecht, C. (2004) 'Using prior information to aid ecological inference: a Bayesian approach', in K. Gary, M. A. Tanner, and O. Rosen (eds) *Ecological Inference: New methodological strategies*, Cambridge: Cambridge University Press, pp. 144–161.

Cowart, A. (1974) 'A cautionary note on aggregate indicators of split ticket voting', *Political Methodology*, 1(1): 109–130.

Cox, G. W. (1997) *Making Votes Count: Strategic coordination in the world's electoral systems*, Cambridge: Cambridge University Press.

Cox, G. W. and Thies, M. F. (2000) 'How much does money matter? "Buying" votes in Japan, 1967-1990', *Comparative Political Studies*, 33(1): 37–57.

Cox, K. E. and Schoppa, L. J. (2002) 'Interaction effects in mixed-member electoral systems', *Comparative Political Studies*, 35(9): 1027–1053.

Curtice, J. (2006) 'A chance to experiment', in C. Bromley, J. Curtice, D. McCrone and A. Park (eds) *Has Devolution Delivered*, Edinburgh: Edinburgh University Press, pp. 109–122.

Cribari-Neto, F. and Zeileis, A. (2010) 'Beta regression in R', *Journal of Statistical Software*, 34(2): 1–24.

D'Alimonte, R. (2003) 'Mixed electoral rules, partisan realignment, and party system change in Italy', in M. Shugart and M. P. Wattenberg (eds) *Mixed-Member Electoral Systems: The best of both worlds*, Oxford: Oxford University Press, pp. 323–350.

— (2005) 'Italy: A case of fragmented bipolarism', in M. Gallagher and P. Mitchell (eds) *The Politics of Electoral Systems*, Oxford: Oxford University Press, pp. 253–276.

Dalton, R. J. (2000) *The Decline of Party Identification*, Oxford University Press.

Darcy, R. and Marsh, M. (1994) 'Decision heuristics: ticket-splitting and the Irish voter', *Electoral Studies*, 13(1): 38–49.

De Sio, L. (2003) 'A proposal for extending King's EI method to mxn tables', available: https://www.academia.edu/906738/A_Proposal_for_Extending_King_s_EI_Method_to_m_n_Tables (accessed July 2015)

— (2009) 'Oltre il modello di Goodman: l'analisi dei flussi elettorali in base a dati aggregati', *Polena*, 1(1): pp. 9–35.

Debus, M. and Müller, J. (2014) 'Expected utility or learned familiarity? The formation of voters' coalition preferences', *Electoral Studies*, 34(1), 54–67.

Di Giovine, A. and Pizzetti, F. (1996) 'Osservazioni sulla nuova legge elettorale per i Consigli regionali', *Le Regioni*, 4: 11–23.

Di Virgilio, A. (2002) 'L'offerta elettorale: la politica delle alleanze si istituzionalizza', in R. D'Alimonte and S. Bartolini (eds) *Maggioritario finalmente? La transizione elettorale 1994-2001*, Bologna: Il Mulino, pp. 79–129.

— (2005) 'The Italian regional elections of April 2005: does the triumph of the Union signal the end of the Berlusconi era?', *South European Society and Politics*, 10(3): 477–490.

— (2007) 'La costruzione dell'offerta politica: progettazione nazionale, realizzazione regionale', in A. Chiaramonte and G. Tarli-Barbieri (eds)

Riforme istituzionali e rappresentanza politica nelle Regioni italiane. Bologna: Il Mulino, pp. 117–144.

Diamanti, I. (2003) *Bianco, rosso, verde... e azzurro: mappe e colori dell'Italia politica*, Bologna: Il Mulino.

Downs, A. (1957) 'An economic theory of political action in a democracy', *The Journal of Political Economy*, 65(2): 135–150.

Duncan, O. and Davis, B. (1953) 'An alternative to ecological correlation', *American Sociological Review*, 18(6): 665–666.

Duverger, M. (1963) *Political Parties: Their organization and activity in the modern state*, New York: J. Wiley.

Elff, M., Gschwend, T. and Johnston, R. (2008) 'Ignoramus, ignorabimus? On uncertainty in ecological inference', *Political Analysis*, 16(1): 70–92.

Elklit, J. and Kjaer, U. (2005) 'Are Danes more inclined to ticket splitting than the Swedes and the English?', *Scandinavian Political Studies*, 28(2): 125–139.

Ferree, K. E. (2004) 'Iterative approaches to $R \times C$ ecological inference problems: where they can go wrong and one quick fix', *Political Analysis*, 12(2): 143–159.

Fiorina, M. (1992) *Divided Government*, New York: Macmillan.

Fisher, S. D. (2004) 'Definition and measurement of tactical voting: the role of rational choice', *British Journal of Political Science*, 34(1): 152–166.

Fisher, S. L. (1973) 'The wasted vote thesis: West German evidence', *Comparative Politics* 5(2): 295–299

Floridia, A. (2005) 'Le nuove leggi elettorali regionali: molte occasioni mancate, alcune novità positive', *Le Regioni*, 33(5): 841–870.

Fortunato, D. and Stevenson, R. T. (2012) 'Perceptions of partisan ideologies: the effect of coalition participation', *American Journal of Political Science*, 57(2), 459–477.

Franklin, M., Niemi, R. and Whitten, G. (1994) 'The two faces of tactical voting', *British Journal of Political Science*, 24(4): 549–557.

Franklin, M. N., van der Eijk, C. and Marsh, M. (1995) 'Referendum outcomes and trust in government: Public support for Europe in the wake of Maastricht', *West European Politics*, 18(3): 101–117.

Fredén, A. (2014) 'Threshold-insurance voting in PR systems: A study of voters' strategic behavior in the 2010 Swedish General Election', *Journal of Elections, Public Opinion and Parties* 24(4): 473–492.

Freedman, D. A., Klein, S. P., Sacks, J., Smyth C.A. and Everett, C.G. (1991) 'Ecological regression and voting rights', *Evaluation Review*, 15(6): 673–711.

Gallagher, M. (1998) 'The political impact of electoral system change in Japan and New Zealand, 1996', *Party Politics*, 4(2): 203–228.

—   (2001) 'The Japanese House of Councillors election 1998 in comparative perspective', *Electoral Studies*, 20(4): 603–625.

Gallagher, M. and Mitchell, P. (2005) 'The mechanics of electoral system' in M. Gallagher and P. Mitchell (eds) *The Politics of Electoral Systems*, Oxford: Oxford University Press, pp. 579–597.

Garrow, D. J. (2012) 'Ruining the house', *The New York Times*, November 13, 2012.

Golder, M. and Stramski, J. (2010) 'Ideological congruence and electoral institutions', *American Journal of Political Science*, 54(1): 90–106.

Golder, S.N. (2005) 'Pre-electoral coalitions in comparative perspective: a test of existing hypotheses', *Electoral Studies*, 24(4): 643–664.

—— (2006) 'Pre-electoral coalition formation in parliamentary democracies', *British Journal of Political Science*, 36(2): 193–212.

Goodman, L. A. (1953) 'Ecological regressions and behavior of individuals', *American Sociological Review*, 18(6): 663–664.

Greiner, J. D., Baines, P. and Quinn, K. M. (2013) 'Package "RxCEcolInf"', available at: http://cran.r-project.org/web/packages/RxCEcolInf/RxCEcolInf.pdf. (accessed July 2014).

Greiner, J. D. and Quinn, K. (2009) 'RxC ecological inference: bounds, correlations, flexibility and transparency of assumptions', *Journal of the Royal Statistical Society: Series A (Statistics in Society)*, 172(1): 67–81.

Gschwend, T. (2007) 'Ticket-splitting and strategic voting under mixed electoral rules: Evidence from Germany', *European Journal of Political Research*, 46(1): 1–23.

Gschwend, T. and Hooghe, M. (2008) 'Should I stay or should I go? An experimental study on voter responses to pre-electoral coalitions', *European Journal of Political Research*, 47(5): 556–577.

Gschwend, T., Johnston, R. and Pattie, C. (2003) 'Split-ticket patterns in mixed-member proportional election systems: estimates and analyses of their spatial variation at the German federal election', *British Journal of Political Science*, 33(1): 109–27.

Haneuse, S. and Wakefield, J. (2004) 'Ecological Inference Incorporating Spatial Dependence' in K. Gary, M. A. Tanner, and O. Rosen (eds) *Ecological Inference: New methodological strategies*, Cambridge: Cambridge University Press, pp. 266–302.

Helmke, G. (2009) 'Ticket splitting as electoral insurance: the Mexico 2000 elections', *Electoral Studies*, 28(1): 70–78.

Herrmann, M. and Pappi, F. U. (2008) 'Strategic voting in German constituencies', *Electoral Studies*, 27(2): 228–244.

Herron, E. S. and Nishikawa, M. (2001) 'Contamination effects and the number of parties in mixed-superposition electoral systems', *Electoral Studies*, 20(1): 63–86.

Herron, M. and Shotts, K. (2003) 'Using Ecological Inference point estimates as dependent variables in second-stage linear regressions', *Political Analysis*, 11(1): 44–64.

Hillygus, D. S. and Jackman, S. (2003) 'Voter decision making in election 2000: campaign effects, partisan activation, and the Clinton legacy', *American Journal of Political Science*, 47(4): 583–596.

Hix, S. and Marsh, M. (2007) 'Punishment or protest? Understanding European Parliament elections', *Journal of Politics*, 69(2): 495–510.

Hobolt, S. B. and Karp, J. A. (2010) 'Voters and coalition governments', *Electoral Studies*, 29(3): 299–307.

Hobolt, S. B., Spoon, J.-J. and Tilley, J. (2009) 'A vote against Europe? Explaining defection at the 1999 and 2004 European Parliament elections', *British Journal of Political Science*, 39(1): 93–115.

Jacobson, G. (1990) 'The effects of campaign spending in House elections: New evidence for old arguments', *American Journal of Political Science*, 34(2): 334–362.

Jesse, E. (1988) 'Split-voting in the Federal Republic of Germany: An analysis of the Federal Elections from 1953 to 1987', *Electoral Studies*, 7(2): 109–124.

Johnston, R. and Pattie, C. (2000) 'Ecological inference and entropy-maximizing: an alternative estimation procedure for split-ticket voting', *Political Analysis*, 8(4): 333–345.

— (2002) 'Campaigning and split-ticket voting in new electoral systems: the first MMP elections in New Zealand, Scotland and Wales', *Electoral Studies*, 21(4): 583–600.

— (2003) 'Spatial variation in straight and split-ticket voting and the role of constituency campaigning: New Zealand's first two MMP elections', *Australian Journal of Political Science*, 38(3): 535–547.

— (2004) 'Switching and splitting: local contexts and campaigns from intentions to the ballot box–New Zealand 1999', *British Elections & Parties Review*, 14(1): 40–71.

— (2006) 'Candidate quality and the impact of campaign expenditure: a British example', *Journal of Elections, Public Opinion and Parties*, 16(3): 283–294.

Kabashima, I. and Reed, S. (2001) 'The effect of the choices available on voting behaviour: the two Japanese elections of 1993', *Electoral Studies*, 20(4): 627–640.

Karp, J. (2006) 'Political knowledge about electoral rules: Comparing mixed member proportional systems in Germany and New Zealand', *Electoral Studies*, 25(4): 714–730.

— (2009) 'Candidate effects and spill-over in mixed systems: Evidence from New Zealand', *Electoral Studies*, 28(1): 41–50.

Karp, J., Vowles, J., Banducci, S. and Donovan, T. (2002) 'Strategic voting, party activity, and candidate effects: testing explanations for split voting in New Zealand's new mixed system', *Electoral Studies*, 21(1): 1–22.

Kato, J. and Kannon, Y. (2008) 'Coalition governments, party switching, and the rise and decline of parties: changing Japanese party politics since 1993', *Japanese Journal of Political Science*, 9(3): 341–365.

Kieschnick, R. and McCullough, B. (2003) 'Regression analysis of variates observed on (0, 1): percentages, proportions and fractions', *Statistical Modelling*, 3(3): 193–213.

King, G. (1997) *A Solution to the Ecological Inference Problem: Reconstructing individual behavior from aggregate data*, Princeton: Princeton University Press.

King, G., Rosen, O. and Tanner, M. (1999) 'Binomial-beta hierarchical models for ecological inference', *Sociological Methods & Research*, 28(1): 61.

— (2004) *Ecological Inference: New methodological strategies*, Cambridge: Cambridge University Press.

Kohno, M. (1997) 'Voter turnout and strategic ticket-splitting under Japan's new electoral rules', *Asian Survey*, 37(5): 429–440.

Kostadinova, T. (2002) 'Do mixed electoral systems matter?: A cross-national analysis of their effects in Eastern Europe', *Electoral Studies*, 21(1): 23–34.

Kramer, G. H. (1983) 'The ecological fallacy revisited: Aggregate-versus individual-level findings on economics and elections, and sociotropic voting', *The American Political Science Review*, 77(1): 92–111.

Liu, B. (2007) 'EI extended model and the fear of ecological fallacy', *Sociological Methods & Research*, 36(1): 3–25.

Long, J. S. (1997) *Regression Models for Categorical and Limited Dependent Variables*, Thousand Oaks, CA: Sage.

McAllister, I. and Darcy, R. (1992) 'Sources of split-ticket voting in the 1988 American elections', *Political Studies*, 40(4): 695–712.

McAllister, I. and White, S. (2000) 'Split ticket voting in the 1995 Russian Duma elections', *Electoral Studies*, 19(4): 563–576.

McKean, M. and Scheiner, E. (2000) 'Japan's new electoral system: la plus ca change...', *Electoral Studies*, 19(4): 447–477.

Maddox, W. and Nimmo, D. (1981) 'In search of the ticket-splitter', *Social Science Quarterly*, 62(3): 401–418.

Magaloni, B. (2004) 'Strategic coordination in the Mexico 2000 presidential race', in: J. I. Domìnguez and C. Lawson (eds) *Mexico's Pivotal Democratic Elections: Candidates, voters, and the presidential campaign of 2000*, California: Stanford University Press, pp. 269–292.

Marsh, M. (2006a) 'Party identification in Ireland: an insecure anchor for a floating party system', *Electoral Studies*, 25(3): 489–508.

— (2006b) 'Stability and change in the structure of electoral competition, 1989–2002', in N. H. J. Garry and D. Payne (eds), *Facing Change in a New Ireland: An analysis of Irish social and political attitudes*, Dublin: Liffey Press, pp. 94–111.

— (2009) 'Vote switching in European Parliament elections: evidence from June 2004', *European Integration*, 31(5): 627–644.

Marsh, M. and Plescia, C. (2015) 'Split-ticket voting in an STV system: choice in a non-strategic context', *Irish Political Studies*, doi:10.1080/07907184.2015.1059323.

Martin, L.W. and Vanberg, G. (2003) 'Wasting time? The impact of ideology and size on delay in coalition formation', *British Journal of Political Science*, 33(2): 323–332.

Mattei, F. and Howes, J. (2000) 'Competing explanations of split-ticket voting in American national elections', *American Politics Research*, 28(3): 379–407.

Meffert, M. F. and Gschwend, T. (2010) 'Strategic coalition voting: evidence from Austria', *Electoral Studies*, 29(3): 339–349.

— (2011) 'Polls, coalition signals and strategic voting: An experimental investigation of perceptions and effects', *European Journal of Political Research*, 50(5): 636–667.

Moser, R. G. and Scheiner, E. (2004) 'Mixed electoral systems and electoral system effects: controlled comparison and cross-national analysis', *Electoral Studies*, 23(4): 575–599.

— (2005) 'Strategic ticket splitting and the personal vote in mixed-member electoral systems', *Legislative Studies Quarterly*, 30(2): 259–276.

Moser, R. G. and Scheiner, E. (2009) 'Strategic voting in established and new democracies: Ticket splitting in mixed-member electoral systems', *Electoral Studies*, 28(1): 51–61.

Niemi, R. G., Written, G. and Franklin, M. N. (1992) 'Constituency characteristics, individual characteristics and tactical voting in the 1987 British general election', *British Journal of Political Science*, 22(2): 229–240.

Norris, P. (2005) 'Political parties and democracy in theoretical and practical perspectives, *National Democratic Institute for International Affairs*, available at: https://www.ndi.org/files/1950_polpart_norris_110105.pdf. (accessed July 2015).

Pacini, M. C. (2007) 'Nuovi (e vecchi) sistemi elettorali regionali', in A. Chiaramonte and G. T. Barbieri (eds) *Riforme istituzionali e rappresentanza politica nelle regioni italiane*, Bologna: Il Mulino, pp. 69–92.

Palda, F. and Palda, K. (1998) 'The impact of campaign expenditures on political competition in the French legislative elections of 1993', *Public Choice*, 94(1-2): 157–174.

Papke, L. and Wooldridge, J. (1996) 'Econometric methods for fractional response variables with an application to 401 (k) plan participation rates', *Journal of Applied Econometrics*, 11(6): 619–632.

Pappi, F. U. and Thurner, P. W. (2002) 'Electoral behaviour in a two-vote system: incentives for ticket splitting in German *Bundestag* elections', *European Journal of Political Research*, 41(2): 207–232.

Park, W., Hanmer, M. J. and Biggers, D. R. (2014) 'Ecological inference under unfavorable conditions: Straight and split-ticket voting in diverse settings and small samples', *Electoral Studies*, 36: 192–203.

Pasquino, G. (1995) *La politica italiana: dizionario critico, 1945-95*, Roma: Laterza.

Pierce, R. (2003) 'Modelling electoral second choices: thwarted voters in the United States, France, and Russia', *Electoral Studies*, 22(2): 265–285.

Powell, G. B. (2009) 'The ideological congruence controversy the impact of alternative measures, data, and time periods on the effects of election rules', *Comparative Political Studies*, 42(12): 1475–1497.

Putnam, R. D. (1993) *Making Democracy Work: Civic traditions in modern Italy*, Princeton: Princeton University Press.

Quinn, K. M. (2004) 'Ecological inference in the presence of temporal dependence', in King, G., Rosen, O. and Tanner M. (eds) *Ecological Inference: New methodological strategies*, Cambridge: Cambridge University Press, pp. 207–232.

Rallings, C. and Thrasher, M. (2001) 'Research note: Measuring the level and direction of split-ticket voting at the 1979 and 1997 British General and Local elections: A survey-based analysis', *Political Studies*, 49(2): 323–330.

— (2003) 'Explaining split-ticket voting at the 1979 and 1997 general and local elections in England', *Political Studies*, 51(3): 558–572.

Rallings, C., Thrasher, M. and Gunter, C. (1998) 'Patterns of voting choice in multi-member districts: the case of English local elections', *Electoral Studies*, 17(1): 111–128.

Reed, S. R. (1999) 'Strategic voting in the 1996 Japanese general election', *Comparative Political Studies*, 32(2): 257–270.

— (2003) (ed.) *Japanese Electoral Politics: Creating a new party system*, London: Nissan Institute/RoutledgeCurzon.

— (2005) 'Japan: haltingly towards a two-party system', in M. Gallagher and P. Mitchell (eds) *The Politics of Electoral Systems*, Oxford: Oxford University Press, pp. 277–293.

Reif, K. (1984) 'National electoral cycles and European elections 1979 and 1984', *Electoral Studies*, 3(3): 244–255.

Reif, K. and Schmitt, H. (1980) 'Nine second-order national elections – A conceptual framework for the analysis of European election results', *European Journal of Political Research*, 8(1): 3–44.

Robinson, W. S. (1950) 'Ecological correlations and the behavior of individuals', *International Journal of Epidemiology*, 38(2): 337–341.

Roscoe, D. D. (2003) 'The choosers or the choices? Voter characteristics and the structure of electoral competition as explanations for ticket splitting', *Journal of Politics*, 65(4): 1147–1164.

Rosen, O., Jiang, W., King, G. and Tanner, M. (2001) 'Bayesian and frequentist inference for ecological inference: the R × C case', *Statistica Neerlandica*, 55(2): 134–156.

Sanz, A. (2008) 'Split-ticket voting in multi-level electoral competition: European, national and regional concurrent elections in Spain', in C. van der Eijk and H. Schmitt (eds) *The Multilevel Electoral System of the EU*, CONNEX Report Series, 04, Mannheim pp. 101–135.

Schoen, H. (1999) 'Split-ticket voting in German Federal elections, 1953-90: an example of sophisticated balloting?', *Electoral Studies*, 18(4): 473–496.

Schoen, H. and Schumann, S. (2007) 'Personality traits, partisan attitudes, and voting behavior: Evidence from Germany', *Political Psychology*, 28(4): 471–498.

Shikano, S., Herrmann, M. and Thurner, P. W. (2009) 'Strategic voting under proportional representation: threshold-insurance in German elections, *West European Politics*, 32(3): 634–656.

Shugart, M. and Wattenberg, M. (2003) *Mixed-Member Electoral Eystems: The best of both worlds?*, Oxford: Oxford University Press.

Shugart, M. S., Valdini, M. E. and Suominen, K. (2005) 'Looking for Locals: Voter Information Demands and Personal Vote-Earning Attributes of Legislators under Proportional Representation', *American Journal of Political Science*, 49(2): 437–49.

Stratmann, T. (2005) 'Some talk: Money in politics, a (partial) review of the literature', *Public Choice*, 124(1-2): 135–56.

Takahashi, Y. 'Explaining split ticket voting in the 2000 federal elections in Mexico, paper presented at the 2004 Meeting of the Latin American Studies Association, Las Vegas (Nevada), October 7-9, 2004.

Tam Cho, W. and Gaines, B. (2004) 'The limits of Ecological Inference: The case of split-ticket voting', *American Journal of Political Science*, 48(1): 152–171.

Tanner, M. A. (1996) *Tools for Statistical Inference*, New York: Springer.

Thomsen, S. R. (1987) *Danish elections 1920-79: A logit approach to ecological analysis and inference*, Aarhus: Politica.

Tsebelis, G. (1986) 'A general model of tactical and inverse tactical voting', *British Journal of Political Science*, 16(3): 395–404.

van der Eijk, C. and Franklin, M. N. (1996) *Choosing Europe?: The European electorate and national politics in the face of union*, University of Michigan Press.

Voss, D. S. (2004) 'Using ecological inference for contextual research: When aggregation bias is the solution as well as the problem', in King, G., Rosen, O. and Tanner, M.(eds) *Ecological inference: New methodological strategies*, Cambridge: Cambridge University Press, pp. 69–96.

Vowles, J. (2005) 'New Zealand: The consolidation of reform?', in M. Gallagher and P. Mitchell (eds) *The Politics of Electoral Systems*, Oxford: Oxford University Press, pp. 295–312.

Wakefield, J. (2004) 'Ecological inference for 2× 2 tables (with discussion)', *Journal of the Royal Statistical Society: Series A (Statistics in Society)*, 167 (3): 385–445.

Wittenberg, J., Alimadhi, F., Lau, O. (2007) 'ei.R XC: hierarchical multinomial-Dirichlet ecological inference model', in Imai, K., King, G., Lau, O. (eds) *Zelig: Everyone's Statistical Software*, available at: http://gking.harvard.edu/zelig. (accessed July 2014)

Wlezien, C. and Erikson, R. S. (2001) 'Campaign effects in theory and practice', *American Politics Research*, 29(5): 419–436.

Wright, G. (1990) 'Misreports of vote choice in the 1988 NES senate election study', *Legislative Studies Quarterly*, 17(1): 113–129.

Zar, J. H. (1996) *Biostatistical Analysis*, Pearson Education India.

Index